CATILINE, THE MONSTER OF ROME

CATILINE

THE MONSTER OF ROME · AN ANCIENT CASE OF POLITICAL ASSASSINATION

FRANCIS GALASSI

WESTHOLME
Yardley

Westholme Publishing, LLC
904 Edgewood Road
Yardley, Pennsylvania 19067
Visit our Web site at www.westholmepublishing.com

First Printing May 2014
10 9 8 7 6 5 4 3 2 1
ISBN: 978-1-59416-196-4
Also available as an eBook.

Printed in the United States of America.

For Caroline

CONTENTS

Contents

PROLOGUE

I MAGINE A GREAT EMPIRE. IT CONTROLS LANDS ACROSS several continents and can influence countries and rulers far away from its borders. Militarily it is the greatest power on Earth, and although it has suffered some setbacks, no one has really defeated it: its eagle remains the undisputed symbol of supremacy. Economically it is far richer than other countries. Technologically it is way ahead of all competitors, and it maintains this position by keeping its doors open to people of different cultures and origins, allowing a free mix of humanity no other country can match. It prizes and protects free speech, religious tolerance, and free political interaction between two powerful parties. It has set up a complex government system made up of elected individuals, and everybody's rights and obligations are spelled out in an original document called the Constitution.

But trouble is brewing in the empire. Its people are increasingly split. On one side is a large, impoverished mass who have lost their traditional jobs and survive thanks to government handouts, or, for young people, by joining the military. On the other side, a small minority of wealthy individuals control the political process and generally display a complete indifference toward those who have less. Games, shows, displays of one sort or another, are put on at appointed times in order to distract the poor. Because the rich keep their own taxation to virtually nothing and the poor have no money, the government of this mighty empire is in a continuous cash crisis. It rules the world while wearing patches on its bottom.

No, this is not the United States of America in the twenty-first century.

This is the Roman Empire in the first century BC.

And this book is the story of a man who tried to reform government and society in Rome and return them to an original equilibrium, however impossible and mythological we may think it was. This man's name has been forgotten, except by specialists; for the record, it was Catiline. His defeat, dramatic and almost romantic to the point that playwrights like Henrik Ibsen and Ben Jonson wrote (not very good) tragedies about it, in effect wiped him off the face of history. Two men in particular brought this about and did all they could to crush Catiline.

One was an ambitious young politician: Gaius Julius Caesar.

The other was an intellectual giant, a man who defined mental categories we still use twenty-one centuries later, who invented words that are on our lips every day, and who clearly saw what measures were necessary for an authoritarian regime to defend itself. Overbearing regimes follow him to this day, whether they know it or not. Besides, he was probably the greatest lawyer of the ancient world: Marcus Tullius Cicero.

Between them, Caesar and Cicero played a perfect *paso doble*: Caesar pushed Catiline to commit political crimes, then denied him support. Cicero used the evidence of criminal behavior to tar Catiline with so many perversions, abuses, and so much corruption that his name became a byword for depravity.

There is only one problem: Caesar deliberately provoked and Cicero knowingly lied to safeguard their own positions. But then, what would you not do if you were trying to protect your power and privileges? Somebody's head has to roll.

This, then, is an attempt to rehabilitate Lucius Sergius Catilina, to pick him out of the mire of lies his detractors pushed him into.

INTRODUCTION

On January 15, 1919, in Berlin, a few men in uniform kidnapped a forty-eight-year-old woman.

Kidnapped, not arrested. The men were not police: they were Freikorps, paramilitary units of veterans of the First World War, set up to quash any attempt at revolution in a defeated, starving, and politically turbulent Germany. When the Freikorps got this woman—and it can't have been difficult, she walked with a limp because of a childhood ailment—only a few months had passed since the Bolsheviks had seized power in Russia, killing Czar Nicholas II and his family, and deposing Prime Minister Aleksander Kerensky. All over Europe, amid strikes, riots, political murders, and street clashes ushered in by a very unsatisfactory war and even more unsatisfactory peace, revolution lurked just around the corner.

In the Freikorps' barracks, the woman was questioned about her participation in a leftist group called

Spartakusbund—Spartacist League. The interrogation was probably harsh: according to medical reports, she may have been beaten with a rifle butt. She certainly was shot in the head by a Freikorps lieutenant, and her body was dumped into the Landwehrkanal, the beautiful waterway that connects Osthafen to Charlottenburg.

The woman's name was Róza Luksemburg.* Polish by birth, she had become a German citizen, changing her name to Rosa Luxemburg. She had worked for the Social Democratic Party but eventually found it too moderate for her political leanings. In 1916, she and several others left the party to found the Spartakusbund, which gave them more scope for hard-line radical propaganda. The league opposed Germany's participation in the war. Luxemburg was repeatedly arrested. She was a marked woman.

But *Spartacus* League? Why Spartacus, the first century BC leader of a gladiator revolt? Luxemburg was a well-educated woman; she had a degree from the University of Zurich, where she had studied philosophy, history, politics, economics, and mathematics. She had specialized in the Middle Ages and economic crises (compare that to the narrow focus of university students today). She must have realized that Spartacus was little more than an assassin. Whatever you may think of her politics, she was intelligent and cultivated. And yet her movement was named after a brutal former soldier and gladiator who had looted and burned and murdered his way up and down Italy, someone who never showed the

*See J. P. Netti, *Rosa Luxemburg* (London: Oxford University Press), 1969, for a life of Luxemburg.

slightest interest or concern for the working classes to which Luxemburg had devoted her life. She could not have been ignorant of Spartacus's deeds. So the question is, why him?

Spartacus was born in 109 BC. He had served as a legionary in the Roman army and proved to be an able military leader. For reasons we do not know today, he was at some point imprisoned and sent to gladiator training school—not a cheering prospect, since it meant you would probably die horribly on the hot sand of an arena for the amusement of a few thousand unemployed. The idea evidently did not appeal to Spartacus, who managed to escape with a group of mates. Unsurprisingly, he quickly turned into little more than a marauder, looting where he could and showing no compassion for people outside his ragtag army. He defeated several Roman expeditionary forces but eventually died at the battle of the River Sele in southern Italy, routed by the legions of Marcus Licinius Crassus, Rome's wealthiest man.

Spartacus was certainly a brave man and a talented soldier, but not a political leader of oppressed masses. And yet, amazingly, over the centuries, he somehow managed to inspire artists and writers and political thinkers like Luxemburg, becoming the symbol of the doomed rebel fighting the good fight against the forces of greed and oppression. None other than Karl Marx himself, in a letter to Friedrich Engels on February 27, 1861, called Spartacus "the most splendid fellow in the whole of ancient history" and a "noble character."

Spartacus's repute does not stop there. In November 2013, a former Black Panther named William Potts returned from Cuba to the United States and was arrested for hijacking a flight from Newark to Miami on March 27, 1984, forcing it to fly to Cuba and demanding a ransom of $5 million. Potts at the time expressed his solidarity with oppressed minorities all over the world. Best of all, he identified himself as "Lt. Spartacus, a soldier in the Black Liberation Army." His choice of nom de guerre reveals that Spartacus was still seen in the late twentieth century as a hero. Potts was at least close to Spartacus in mindset: like his namesake, he tried to extract money by threats and violence. Black Panthers aside, to this very day, football teams, books, music scores, ballets, plays, computer games, and Hollywood movies bear Spartacus's name. Even a mountain has been named Spartacus, not an honor often associated with gladiators.* If you visit the Louvre museum in Paris, you can admire a seven-foot statue of Spartacus by Denis Foyatier in the Puget courtyard. Arthur Koestler wrote a novel (*The Gladiators*) in honor of Spartacus. The myth lives on.

A year after Spartacus's birth, another little boy was born. He was the last descendant of a somewhat impoverished aristocratic family in Rome and was named Lucius Sergius Catilina. Unlike Spartacus, Catilina, or Catiline, as he is referred to in English, was a true revolutionary. After spending his youth in close association with extremely conservative groups, he had the courage

---

*The mountain is a 2,132-foot peak in the Delchev Ridge of the Tangra Mountains, in eastern Livingston Island, in the South Shetland Islands, Antarctica. A chilly place for a man who spent all his life in the Mediterranean.

to review his political ideas and eventually planned a revolutionary attack to bring about a complete upheaval of the greedy and corrupt Roman society of his time. He recruited the poor, the dispossessed, and (horror!) many women. He was actually much closer, politically and morally, to Luxemburg than Spartacus ever could be. And one trait he had in common with Spartacus: Catiline was a good soldier.

And yet if he is remembered at all, Catiline is viewed as a dubious character at best, if not actually some kind of depraved monster. One of the kinder descriptions comes from the Oxford English Dictionary, which, under his name, has this entry: "The name of a Roman who in BC 63 conspired against his country: sometimes taken as the type of a profligate conspirator."

Already saying someone "conspired" is pretty damning. And "against his country"? This adds the heavy suspicion of treason. Plus, "profligate." We are talking real darkness. A money-wasting traitor who plotted to bring down his country. Holding him in Guantánamo Bay would be too good for him.

This book argues that Catiline was none of those things. Yes, he plotted to tear up the corrupt Rome he had been born into. He developed a plan and meant to carry it through to the end, but he had very limited resources. In the end, he was stopped by those same moneyed upper classes he had defended in one of Rome's many civil wars. And in stopping him, Cicero, who was an opportunistic provincial lawyer and politician, described him as a perverted, immoral conspirator in words that the Oxford English Dictionary is still repeating, twenty-one centuries later.

The portrait that we have of Catiline ensured that Luxemburg and her associates could not even consider naming their league after him. They needed a hero to inspire their followers, and even to educated minds, Catiline was not a hero but a corrupt, violent, and depraved madman. The author of Catiline's damnation and infamy through the centuries was Marcus Tullius Cicero.

Two more characters played their part in Catiline's life. The first we have already met: Marcus Licinius Crassus, Rome's wealthiest man, who could buy and sell political favors as if they were peanuts. The other was not very well known at the time, though he is nowadays seen as the very personification of Roman power: Gaius Julius Caesar.

Of the three, we know Cicero's views of Catiline, and know them in detail (he was never one to shut up). Crassus did not write anything, so we can only suspect that for him, Catiline was a pawn. Caesar wrote plenty, but not once does he mention Catiline. And from Catiline himself we have only a very dignified letter asking a friend to look after his wife, sent a few days before he died in battle.

That was in January 62 BC.

A Note on Roman Names

Ancient Romans in Catiline's time had three names (a bit like T. S. Eliot's cats). These were the *praenomen*, *nomen*, and *cognomen*. Let's see what each meant, using our protagonist: Lucius (praenomen) Sergius (nomen) Catilina (cognomen).

The praenomen, Lucius, was reserved for the family or close friends. You would be Lucius to your parents, your siblings, your aunts and uncles and cousins, as well as your playmates. It's what we would call a first name.

The nomen, Sergius, identified you as a member of a family and, therefore, gave your origins, your lineage, and your status. The family we are talking about was an extended family—indeed, some of these families included hundreds of people. They were the gens, which some historians translate as "tribe" or "clan." But this way of putting things is misleading and creates confusion with another Roman use of the word "tribe" we shall meet later. The word "gens" is related to our verb "generate": the gens were the people who could trace their origins to the founder of the family, the man whose descendants they were. (Man, not woman: women came under the gens of the husband and contributed their reproductive power to his gens. "Gens" is also the root of our modern words "genetics" and "genitals.") Now an important detail: the word "gens" is (strangely, given the Romans' views on the matter) grammatically feminine, so that you talk about the "gens Sergia"—descendants of Sergius—even though the subject of this book was a man (Lucius Sergius). Usually words ending in "a" were feminine in Latin, those ending in "us" masculine, and any other ending could be either. But not necessarily.

More importantly, the name of the gens was linked to the founding families of Rome, the old aristocracy of the city. The gens Sergia claimed to derive from Sergestus, one the followers of Aenaeas, the warrior-prince who had escaped from Troy when the Greeks were putting it to the torch and, after a lot of meandering around the Mediterranean, fetched up on the Italian shore. This bit of family lore matters a great deal in Catiline's story.

Finally, the cognomen: this is the trickiest bit because we have no modern equivalent. But imagine a gens of dozens of people. You would need to distinguish Lucius Sergius son of Silo from Lucius Sergius son of Marcus. The cognomen linked people of the same gens to different specific ancestors, all of whom were born within the same gens. It was a way of saying, "I am one of Silo's great-great-grandchildren and you're one of Marcus's, and both Silo and Marcus descend from Sergius." The cognomen may then become the name by which one was generally known: Catiline, oh yes, one of the Silo branch of the gens Sergia. But here we run into a problem: the cognomen Catilina is unique in Roman history. Nobody else, not in the gens Sergia (Catiline's family) nor in any other gens, seems to have borne it. Ever. Does this mean it was the nickname of this particular individual? That is not impossible: in Latin, *catulus* meant "small dog," so "Catiline" might in fact mean "doglike," indicating doglike strength, or aggressiveness, or resistance. All of these would match the historian Sallust's description of Catiline as having an extraordinary ability to "endure hunger, cold, and want of sleep." Or could it be that it was the name of a smaller branch of the gens Sergia whose name left no trace in history books and was picked up again by Catiline's father as a gesture of respect for a dead branch of the family? We simply do not know.

A Note on Geographical Names

At the time Catiline lived, the name Italia was applied to a smaller area than what we call Italy. To the Romans, Italia was the territory south of the river Rubicon (see map). North of that, the valley of the Po and the foothills of the Alps, inhabited by Gaulish tribes, were called Gallia Cisalpina, Gaul within the Alps. South of the Rubicon, the population was called Italici, "the Italic people" or "the people of Italia." I will use this geographic arrangement because it reflects reality at the time, even though it is different from today's borders and names.

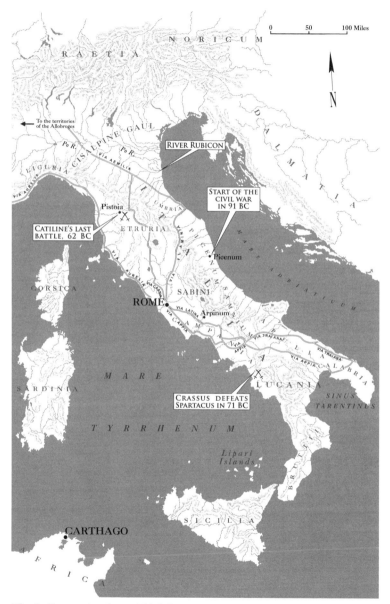

The Italian peninsula, c. 100 BC.

Rome, 100 BC

The Rome into which Catiline was born was not a peaceable place.

The city had grown immensely in power and wealth in the previous century or so.* Less than forty years before Catiline's birth, Rome had defeated its long-standing rival, Carthage (in what is today's Tunisia), flattened the city, and poured tons of salt on the few remaining ruins so nothing would ever again grow near them, which, even by the much more murderous standards of the twentieth century, was somewhat brutal. The

---

*This chapter relies on Jérôme Carcopino, *Cicero: The Secrets of His Correspondence* (New York: Routledge & Kegan Paul, 1951); C. M. Mommsen, *Römische Geschichte,* 3 vols. (Leipzig, Germany: Reimer & Hirsel, 1854–1856); and Mikhail Ivanovich Rostovtzeff, *Social and Economic History of the Roman Empire* (New York: Biblo & Tannen, 1926).

Romans had also enslaved the whole surviving population, which is nowadays reckoned at fifty thousand people. In the process, Rome had acquired territories in Spain, Africa, and pretty well all of the Mediterranean islands, to complement its possessions in Greece, Turkey, and on the eastern coast of the Adriatic. The defeat of Carthage marked the beginning of Roman superpower status, which would last over six centuries and spread the Roman alphabet, Roman speech, Roman institutions, and, in the long run, Christianity, all over Europe, eventually passing each of them on to European colonies all over the world. It was one of those moments when history went one way and closed the door on other outcomes.

Whatever the long-term results, the benefits of these conquests were not evenly spread across the Roman population. The powerful men who commanded the troops in effect seized the properties located in the conquered lands and started farming them with slaves—often the very people who had been defeated. These properties were supposed to belong to the Roman state, but who was going to pick a fight with a general backed up by a well-trained and experienced army? So the land that was supposed to provide income for the government (no income tax existed) instead financed the extravagant lifestyle of a powerful elite.

Farming with slaves had a big advantage: it was cheap, especially since Rome's continuous wars ensured that slaves were always in plentiful supply. The result was that the rapidly expanding lands of the very rich yielded grain, fruit, vegetables, wine, oil, and meat, in direct competition with what small farmers could bring to market. One after the other, the small farmers fell into debt, eventually went under, sold their farms for a few coins, and moved to the cities. In particular, they moved to Rome, where free distributions of grain were organized by the government (run by the same people whose landholdings provided competition to the small farmers). Also, in Rome, some kind of menial job could always be found, and some rich man was always willing to drop a few coins into your hand in return for running an errand. Or voting for him—because, you see, Rome was a democracy, and public offices could only be filled by free and fair elections.

The same thing happened to small artisans, who had sold their goods (shoes, farm tools, cloth, earthenware, metalwork) to the farmers. Their customers moved away, and any who were left would supply their needs from the wares manufactured by slave labor. Like the farmers before them, artisans eventually shut up shop and moved to Rome.

As Roman power grew, the population of Rome was ever more split between a rich class of owners of large estates and an impoverished, parasitical mass. And here lies the tale.

Many of the new rich had no gens; they had simply been clever or lucky to grab lands in this or that campaign. They were not used to the idea, common among the old aristocracy, that wealth and power confer responsibilities toward the poor. They despised the poor, something that would have been inconceivable to the old aristocrats. The sense of noblesse oblige had among the old nobility a strange power, almost a grip that could not be shaken off. The nouveaux riches had no sense of that, and in fact wanted to distinguish themselves from the impoverished masses from which they had just emerged. Let the poor drown in their own filth.

Except, of course, when it came to voting. Then it was different.

Some of the nouveaux riches had set up vast financial institutions that lent to poor farmers and, when they could not repay, seized their land. They also lent to people who wanted to finance a political career, which was very expensive: think of all the impoverished would-be voters who came around selling their support in exchange for a bit of gold. If as financier you picked the right politicians, the return on your lending could be beyond all expectations. And if you played your cards right, you could influence legislation or, more importantly, its application. As I said, this was, after all, a democracy.

Growing inequality and the open abuse of the law could not last without strife. In the years around Catiline's birth, there were a number of revolts by the Roman lower classes against this unending, growing inequality between rich and poor. The problem was not new: about four centuries earlier, most of the Roman poor had walked out of the city in a kind of general strike meant to ensure that measures would be put in place to guarantee the poor's protection. They did win some reforms, but reforms have to be administered by human beings, and human beings have a price. However, the most important reform the poor wanted, land redistribution, simply did not go through. The aristocracy and rich landowners blocked it, at times resorting to open murder; for example, the brothers Gaius and

Tiberius Gracchus, who had pushed for land reform, were both assassinated around twenty years before Catiline's birth. Over the long term, whatever reforms were won ended up amounting to very little.

The year after Catiline was born, a man named Gaius Marius was elected as a Roman consul—in effect, the executive power in the city. Marius did not come from a founding gens; his was from what we would call the provincial middle class. His election to such high office would normally have been very unlikely, but Marius had some money of his own and had hit on a fruitful campaign trick: he thundered against the army general who was currently fighting one of Rome's many foreign wars, in this case against Germanic tribes named the Teutones, the Ambrones, and the Cymbri. Marius accused the general of corruption, incompetence, and lack of drive in the war. The charge resonated with the poor, and Marius was elected.

He ran again the following year, even though it was illegal to have two terms in office, and again won. His street gangs managed to intimidate voters so much that Marius was reelected over and over, setting up a virtual dictatorship. As new general of the army, he also brought the war against the Teutones, Ambrones, and Cymbri to a successful conclusion. Shortly after that, he defeated other Germanic tribes that had slaughtered a Roman army sent to oppose them. He returned to Rome bearing the eagle standards of his victorious legions and was given a triumphal procession through the city.

As supreme commander, he also reorganized the army, transforming the traditional conscripts into semi-professional soldiers, introducing bigger and more flexible battle formations, and improving the equipment and training: in effect, he made the legions much more efficient and aggressive. Though the poor idolized him, in good part because his army reforms had opened up long-term employment for many young men, the aristocracy viewed him with deep suspicion but dared not oppose him. As Marius ran for consul in election after election, his victories, based as they were on the intimidation of street gangs, were resented, even aside from the illegality of Marius's action. Marius's arrogance in selecting a running partner for the other office of consul (there were always two consuls), letting it be known who this was and ensuring his election thanks to the street gangs that followed him, was insulting to the members of the older gens. Once in office yet again, Marius would assign his colleague to deal with minor matters, in a sense showing the aristocrats just what he thought of them.

Other than his repeated elections to the office of consul (though no one dared oppose him), Marius had trouble in the long run capitalizing on the goodwill of the poor. He remained the virtual boss of the city for almost twenty years but was hated by the moneyed aristocracy, and that eventually led to a terrifying civil war. Before then, however, he ran Rome unopposed, frightening the aristocracy and relying on two dubious characters—Lucius Appuleius Saturninus and Gaius Servilius Glaucia—whose abuses and violence were turning people against him, both the poor and the better off. Eventually his supporters' brutality brought about his own downfall.

Saturninus and Glaucia were thugs: they intimidated, beat, and murdered anyone they felt might pose a threat to Marius and, therefore, to their own positions as gang leaders. Rome trembled as these gangs acted with complete impunity, maintaining a reign of petty terror in the streets. The situation lasted until the Senate, not yet entirely under a dictator's thumb, intervened. As consul, it was Marius's responsibility to restore order in the city, which meant taking his street gangs in hand. When the Senate told him to get on with it, he was clever enough to see the straws in the wind. He decided to obey the Senate's injunction and abandoned Saturninus and Glaucia, on whom he had relied to be illegally reelected over and over. These two were surrounded and murdered by a furious mob of poor people who had had enough of abuse and arbitrary rule.

It is important to remember who the poor people of Rome were: impoverished farmers and artisans. Some had been ruined by the competition of large estates or workshops run with slave labor, but others were ex-soldiers who had been farmers or artisans. Before Marius's reforms, the Roman army provided only minimal uniforms or kit for its soldiers; pretty well everything had to be brought along by the soldier himself. Richer men were expected to come with a horse, the poorer on foot. The army paid only a minimal salary, and the result was that for a family of small farmers or artisans, sending a man to war was a considerable expense. They hoped to gain from it if the soldier (assuming he survived the war) was given land by the victorious general. But in the meanwhile, the family had to eat somehow, and that was when the moneylenders appeared. The families financed their needs until the next harvest, and waited.

Even under the best circumstances, a farmer's family missing a male member—more exactly, a young male member—would have a hard time producing what it needed. The slightest bad weather or crop parasite would sink it. If the farmers could not pay then, the artisans who produced for them were equally in financial trouble. At this point, repaying a moneylender would be out of the question. Soon the farmers' or artisans' land or workshop passed out of their possession to the moneylenders. That added to the number of urban poor.

If, to top it all, a man who had gone to war had been wounded so as to be unable to work, or if the war had not gone as well as hoped, or other veterans had been better placed to seize the best land, urban destitution was assured. It is important to understand what that meant: the public authorities took no responsibility for the fate or living conditions of the Roman poor, outside of the free distributions of grain that encouraged a mindset of economic and psychological dependency. If we can dismiss from our minds the images of gleaming marbles and golden statues that are associated with ancient Rome (they were there, but at a later date), the best way to picture the city in these years is a vast urban center of jerry-built wooden houses with rotting garbage in the streets, where refuse was thrown out of windows into filthy streams that ran down the middle of the road. Yes, there were well-developed sewers, running water in fountains at the corners of the streets, magnificent roads, bridges, aqueducts, harbors, and waterworks throughout the empire. But Rome itself was a mess, and eventually, as the city choked in its own filth and chaos, traffic and health regulations were adopted.

In the midst of this debris and destitution, amid the smells of rotting garbage, in a grinding poverty such as today we can only observe in cities of the Third World, the vast majority of the people, impoverished and indebted though they were, retained one source of pride. It was an unquestionable pride, a sense of belonging to the greatest power the world had ever seen. They were Roman citizens.

They were Roman citizens. The sea itself had bent to their will—they called it *mare nostrum* ("our sea")—as if it had been a lake on which they could sail at their pleasure. And this they could do because each of them was a *civis Romanus.*

The issue of citizenship had been festering for a while and eventually led to yet another civil war. The Italic populations wanted to be Roman citizens for a number of reasons. First, it meant being somewhat sheltered against abuses by Roman dignitaries and officers. Second, it meant having easier access to the courts when seeking redress against some wrong done to them by a Roman citizen. Last, and most important, citizenship meant enjoying the right to vote and elect those people who decided issues that mattered to the Italic populations subject to Roman rule. The big issue here was war: these populations, by the first century BC, formed the core of the Roman army, but they had no say in where, when, and whom they fought. They wanted Roman citizenship because it gave them political heft.

In practice, though, the right to vote was difficult to exercise: polling only took place in Rome itself, in mid- to late summer, and most people simply could not afford to undertake a long and costly trip. Besides, the voting did not take place under a system of proportional representation. So the Italic people could be packed together in a few constituencies that would make no difference in the actual result most of the time (more on this later). The right to vote, then, was theoretical, but it could become practical if there was an issue of great importance, at which point the Italic votes would have swamped those of the residents of the city even if the extra voters were packed in a handful of constituencies. This did happen when Catiline ran for office in 63 BC.

Exactly for this reason, the Roman poor were dead set against the extension of Roman citizenship. If many more voters had been rattling about the streets, the urban poor could only expect smaller bribes from the candidates. The urban poor lived on these handouts and were not willing to share them, even if that was likely to happen only in exceptional circumstances. But the fear was there.

The tensions between the Italic peoples and Rome were rising throughout Catiline's youth. In summer 92 BC, the streets of Rome were full of Italic peoples who had traveled to the city and loudly demonstrated for their right to become Roman. The Roman poor reacted, and there were clashes and deaths. The Senate did nothing. Eventually, in 91 BC, the pressure became too great: in a town on the east coast of Italia called Picenum (today's Ascoli Piceno), the population attacked and slaughtered thousands of Roman citizens. It was a call to arms for the Italic peoples and a declaration of war to Rome.

That same year, having just turned eighteen, Catiline was called up for military service. This is the first report we have of his life.

2

THE GOVERNMENT
OF ROME

L ET'S LEAVE CATILINE IN THE ARMY RECRUITMENT office for the moment, and let's look instead at how the government of Rome worked in his time. Everything that was about to happen to him depended on the political arrangements of the Roman state. If these arrangements are already familiar to you, bear with me, as this chapter may throw a different light on the Roman state.

The first point to keep in mind is that the Romans understood only one source of power, which they called *imperium*. The imperium belonged to the totality of the Roman population—well, no, women had no imperium, neither did slaves or minors, but if you were a Roman adult male, you shared in the collective imperium with all other Roman adult males. If you were an adult male of one of the Italic peoples, sorry, you did not share in the imperium (there were a few exceptions, but they do not matter in our story). The idea that individuals had rights that could not be violated never entered the Roman mind: you might well have a right to be judged by other Roman citizens, but this right was the result of the fact that *you* were a Roman citizen. Otherwise, no.

In addition, saying that the Romans understood only one source of power means something much more fundamental, at least to our way of thinking: the imperium was one and only one. It could not be divided. If that seems like playing with words, it isn't. It means that the distinction we draw between legislative power, executive power, and judicial power did not exist as a principle in the Roman world. You could be judged by a legislative assembly, have a legislative and judicial role while acting as a member of the executive, and so on. To the Romans, there was nothing incompatible here, as there would be to us if a judge was also prime minister or president. The idea of checks and balances in which each of the three powers restrains the activities of the others was not part of their mental structure. Of course, specific functions would be fulfilled by different individuals: a senator had no time to attend (say) a court case that did not involve him, so someone else had to be delegated as judge, but even so, that person exercised imperium. The separation was administrative, but in the end power was power. Checks and balances applied to relations between groups (rich and poor, say) but not to branches of the government. Over the centuries, some offices were set up to prevent abuse in specific actions by other officials, but it was the reaction to specific events, never a fundamental organizing principle as it is, for example, in the US Constitution. Needless to say, this reaction to specific abuses was itself open to abuse, and many political scores were settled by introducing laws that only dealt with one specific case involving one's particular political opponent.

The result was that by Catiline's time, the Roman state was a hodgepodge of rules, offices, rights, and obligations that had accumulated over the centuries. The only way to understand this is to briefly follow its history. The starting point is the end of the monarchy in 510 BC and the setting up of the republic (from the Latin *res publica*, the people's business). The republic started out with a legislative assembly called the Senate (the name derives from *senes*, aged person, so the Senate was the elders' council), made up of the heads of the founding gens of Rome—the gens Julia, gens Flaminia, gens Cornelia, gens Sergia, and so on. These were the aristocracy of the republic, known as the *optimates* (the leading ones). The Senate made foreign and domestic policy and generally supervised the functioning of the government. Although it was made up of aristocrats, we must not think of it as a conservative stronghold: the optimates ranged across the full extent of the political spectrum.

The Senate also held the purse strings, and no public money could be spent without its approval. In addition, it functioned as a kind of high court, trying individuals accused of particularly heinous crimes, such as treason. By law, all debate—though not necessarily a vote—had to be finished by nightfall on the day a motion had been introduced, and senators spoke on a motion in order of seniority. If you were good at public speaking, you could therefore talk a proposal to death by just speaking about it until the sun set (or hiring someone to do it for you).

Side by side with the Senate were two assemblies, the Comitia Centuriata and the Comitia Tributa. These assemblies met yearly in the summer and elected what we could call executive officials: the Centuriata elected higher officials of the state, such as consuls, *praetores*, and *censores,* while the Tributa elected lower officials, such as *quaestores* and the *aediles.**

The election mechanism was important: in neither assembly did you vote individually. You voted as part of a group.

In the Centuriata you voted as a member of your *centuria,* the army unit into which you were enrolled, for life, at age eighteen. In the Tributa, you voted according to your tribe, which really meant the section of the city where you lived. To be in the army you had to own at least a certain amount of property. This meant that the Centuriata was the more conservatively inclined of the two assemblies, if for no other reason than because it grouped together the aristocracy as commanders of most centuria, and who would challenge the will of their commanding officer in a matter of voting? Even without that, the sample of the Roman population from which the Centuriata was drawn had larger property holdings than the population as a whole, so it is not surprising that it would gravitate to what we would call the political Right.

---

*The consuls had supreme civil and military power. The praetores administered civil law, presided over the courts, and commanded provincial armies. The censores conducted a census on the basis of which they could appoint people to the Senate. The aediles managed domestic policy in Rome, including controlling the markets and public games. The quaestores were financial officers for the consuls in Rome and for provincial governors.

The Comitia Centuriata reveal their ancient origin as the assembly of the people in arms. The Centuriata would discuss political decisions and elect their commanders, the two consuls and the six praetores. These officials played a role that was generally executive of government policy and included supreme military command for the consuls. This meant, by the principle of the imperium, that the Comitia Centuriata also had a legislative role, and even a judicial one. It also established a rough equality among voters, since they all voted in army units made up of the same number of soldiers (centuria, one hundred), so that at least in the Centuriata, each man had the same voting power. But that power was diluted, since each man voted as part of an army unit, and only the overall vote of each army unit counted in the Centuriata outcome. Still, the Centuriata had at least an appearance of democracy.

No such rough equality existed in the Comitia Tributa. This assembly depended on the tribe to which each citizen was assigned, which more often than not meant where he lived. Every Roman male belonged to a tribe, so at least in this way the Tributa was more inclusive than the Centuriata. But you voted by tribe, not individually: if your tribe had a thousand members and mine had only ten, my vote counted one hundred times more than yours. Even so, the Tributa provided the poor with an assembly where they were in a better position to make their voices heard: given the disproportion between poor and aristocrats, chances were that most tribes had a majority of poor voters. And if a majority of tribes voted for a measure, the measure was adopted.

Even so, the legislative and executive powers of the Centuriata and the Senate remained awesome, and the Tributa could not always be counted on to support initiatives in favor of the poor (or believed to be such). It was in 494 BC, less than twenty years after the end of the monarchy, that the Roman poor, tired of the unrestrained power of the aristocracy, left the city and set up camp on a hill nearby. In return for resuming their normal tasks they insisted that they, as poor and not simply as members of the Tributa, should have the right to elect their own officials, and that these should be able to veto laws and initiatives that the Comitia or the Senate were examining. The aristocracy gave in: in the fifth century BC, the poor of Rome still played an important economic and military function, and without them the city had come to a standstill.

The innovation came in the form of two officials called tribunes, elected annually by the poor of the Comitia Tributa. The tribunes had, on paper, considerable power: they could veto any act passed by the Comitia Centuriata, the Comitia Tributa, or the Senate. In addition, since the poor were wise to the ways of the aristocracy, the two tribunes were made "personally inviolate"—you could not touch them, never mind kill them—and their intervention in legislative and policy matters had to be accepted under penalty of capital punishment.

In principle this almost transformed Rome into a tribune-led dictatorship. In practice that never happened. The tribunes could be managed, flattered, bribed. The richer ones could be eased into the ranks of the aristocracy simply by introducing them to other aristocrats,

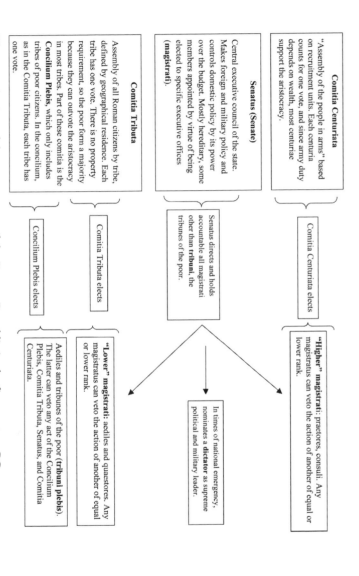

Comitia Centuriata

"Assembly of the people in arms" based on recruitment units. Each centuria counts for one vote, and since army duty depends on wealth, most centuriae support the aristocracy.

Senatus (Senate)

Central executive council of the state. Makes foreign and military policy and controls domestic policy by its power over the budget. Mostly hereditary, some members appointed by virtue of being elected to specific executive offices (**magistrati**).

Comitia Tributa

Assembly of all Roman citizens by tribe, defined by geographical residence. Each tribe has one vote. There is no property requirement, so the poor form a majority in most tribes. Part of these comitia is the **Concilium Plebis**, which only includes tribes of poor citizens. In the concilium, as in the Comitia Tributa, each tribe has one vote.

Comitia Centuriata elects

Senatus directs and holds accountable all magistrati other than **tribuni**, the tribunes of the poor.

Comitia Tributa elects

Concilium Plebis elects

"**Higher**" **magistrati:** praetores, consuli. Any magistratus can veto the action of another of equal or lower rank.

In times of national emergency, nominates a **dictator** as supreme political and military leader.

"**Lower**" **magistrati:** aediles and quaestores. Any magistratus can veto the action of another of equal or lower rank.

Aediles and tribunes of the poor (**tribuni plebis**). The latter can veto any act of the Concilium Plebis, Comitia Tributa, Senatus, and Comitia Centuriata.

The organization of the government of the Roman Republic in the first century BC.

helping them strike business deals, helping them with loan and credit transactions, guaranteeing their solvency, and similar methods. If all else failed, they could be offered a patrician daughter in marriage. Co-opted tribunes may well have thought in terms of their duty to protect the interests of the poor, but this became ever more difficult as the Senate refined its ability to draw the tribunes toward itself.

For those who did not bite the carrot, there were nice, strong sticks. Perhaps the best known individuals to feel just how heavy those sticks could be were Gaius and Tiberius Gracchus, two brothers who, some years apart, ran for and won the office of tribune, from which they proposed landownership reforms. Mysteriously, in 132 BC, Gaius was attacked by an unidentified mob and murdered together with several of his followers. Ten years later, Tiberius also died with hundreds of his supporters in unclear circumstances. But Tiberius had also made a major political blunder that had alienated the poor of Rome: he had proposed the extension of Roman citizenship to the Italic peoples. It would be difficult to find a surer way to alienate his supporters. Nobody was ever tried for the murders.

The last important office in all this was the dictator, a supreme military and civil commander appointed by the consuls on instructions from the Senate. This was an extraordinary step, taken only in times of grave danger. The appointment was for six months and could be renewed. Interestingly, the dictator was not legally liable for his actions while in office, whereas all other officials were—evidence again that the appointment was seen as an unusual measure during an emergency. With time, this office, too, was abused, and people had themselves reappointed dictator for fabricated emergencies just in order to retain power.

Roman public life had a few more twists. The first was that even as a Roman citizen, you were not free to put forth your candidacy for any office you liked. There was a specific order in which you could run for office, and it was designed to mix civilian and military posts so as to give the future consuls a wide experience of government and military matters. This order was called the *cursus honorum* (route of offices). The cursus started with military duty, followed by the candidacy for quaestor, then aedilis, praetor, and consul. Note that this did not include election to the office of tribune of the poor, which was not, strictly speaking, an office of the government but a political agency designed to monitor the power of consuls, both Comitia, and the Senate.

Each office in the cursus was subject to minimum age requirements, from thirty for quaestor to forty-two for consul. Also, you could not run for an office you had already held—though we have seen that efficient street gangs could make sure this did not apply to you. A minimum amount of time had to elapse before you could put forth your candidacy for the next step. You did this by wearing a bleached garment, the *toga candida*, which identified you as a *candidatus* (candidate) and symbolized the purity of your intentions and your ethics— which was a bit of a joke, given the reality of Roman politics, the ease with which rules were flouted, and the accommodating nature of those who were in charge of enforcing the law. One of the most egregious examples of this was, as we have seen, the popular leader Gaius

Marius, who was reelected consul seven times because his followers so terrified the Senate that nobody dared say anything.

But even without going to such extremes, ensuring that people voted for you was costly. You would have underlings (who had to be paid) who would pass cash to members of the Comitia Centuriata or Tributa. To have a shot at the higher offices, you had to organize public games, finance shows at religious festivals, set up free distribution of bread or oil or wine, and generally throw money around to prove your affection for the voters. You basically had to indebt yourself up to your neck to maintain a small army of underlings and minions (*clientes*) who would gather at your house every morning, expecting to earn their lunch thanks to your tips, doing the small favors you asked of them, running the errands you sent them on. Among these were rustling up support for you, including gathering the admiring crowd surrounding and cheering you as you strode through the streets in your toga candida that proclaimed to all what a morally upright person you were. Your clients had a fine nose for the political scents, and a candidate who could not spend enough to convince members of the assemblies to vote for him would soon find himself alone. It was a vicious game.

At the end of a political career, or even just during the time until you could again be a candidate for a higher step in the cursus, if you had survived legal actions, plots to assassinate you, disqualification on actual or trumped-up charges, or even simply the collapse of your credit rating, you were rewarded with the governorship of a conquered province. That was payback time.

There was no guarantee that a governorship would restore what you had spent in your political career, but in practice it was accepted that as a governor, you had a certain latitude in taxing the population and pocketing some of the revenue, imposing new duties, seizing property of people who had opposed Roman rule, enslaving people who had rebelled and selling them, getting a cut on the cost of public works (roads, aqueducts, bridges, harbors), and applying all the manifold ways by which people in positions of authority benefit their private welfare. This was not considered, as we would think, a form of corruption: it was the application of imperium, Rome's right to govern its conquered lands simply because it had conquered them. Of course, you had to do it with a certain amount of discretion, even style. No mass spoliation, no wholesale confiscations, no grand murder or larceny. The rule seems to have been, "Make them pay taxes, keep them quiet, and don't break the bank." Unless, of course, the whole population rioted, in which case you could bring in the legions and then no holds were barred: crucifixion for the men, enslavement for the women and children.

But short of that, Rome seems to have expected its governors to act in the interest of maintaining a peaceful equilibrium within its empire. This Pax Romana (Roman Peace) may at times have been oppressive, but overall it was manifested as a device to ensure that conquered provinces accepted the benefits of Roman rule without causing trouble. To do that, you had to show that anyone who broke ranks would receive a thrashing they would not likely forget. Power flows from the barrel of a gun, as another empire builder said. Or from the blade of a *gladius* (the short sword of the Roman legion) in our case.

After you had spent your time as governor of some forsaken province of this suddenly grown empire, you went back to Rome, where, if you were seen as a threat, someone would come after you with allegations, lawsuits, or, if you were really unlucky, groups of thugs waiting around the corner. That someone, needless to say, was another candidate for the same next office in the cursus as you could aspire to. You would protect yourself in the same way, and meet murdering mob with murdering mob. If you survived, you could run for office. If you had any money left, that is.

There was another feature to the Roman political system that is important to our story: in the beginning, the Roman population was divided in *orders*, that is, classes based on family. The gens were, by and large, identified with the optimates, and those without aristocratic backgrounds were the *populares*. But as society changed, orders changed. This is an important side of Catiline's life.

By the time of his birth, a new order had come into existence. It was called the equestrian order (*equites*) and had its roots in a fiscal problem. In the early years, the Senate paid for horses that were needed in time of war. But early wars were reasonably small-scale affairs fought rather close to Rome. Around 400 BC, as more and more territory was conquered, distances grew, and the army—and with it the cavalry—became a bigger enterprise. The Senate simply found it could not financially keep up. Cavalry was not a terribly important part of the Roman army in this period, but you had to have a few riders galloping about, harassing opposing troops, pursuing stragglers, and generally intimidating the enemy. Their usefulness was limited by the curious fact that the Romans, fantastic engineers though they were, never developed or used the stirrup. It's not easy to sit on a galloping horse without stirrups and harass enemy troops.

In any event, stirrups or no stirrups, the optimates would not play around with horses: their military tradition was to fight on foot among the ranks of their men (and their voters, come to it). The disappearing public cavalry, victim of fiscal prudence and budget cuts, was replaced by the rich populares, who supplied privately financed horses, together with equipment and food. In return for providing this service, they insisted on being recognized as a separate order, the equestrian order.

The equestrians were the richest, possibly the most aggressive, among the populares, and they took this opportunity to establish their social advancement, in the process becoming perhaps the most conservative of the three orders. Distinguishing themselves from the poor populares was essential because it suggested wealth and prowess. But it is important to note that being recognized as an equestrian did not change your political status. You still belonged to the same Centuriata and Tributa as before, and voted with them, your vote counting neither more nor less than before. However, you had now acquired, in a sense, the strange position of swing vote. There were enough of you to tip the voting in the Centuriata and Tributa toward the populares. This mattered little in the Centuriata, where the optimates had a clear leadership for the reasons we have seen. But it could matter quite a bit in the Tributa, where the aristocratic majority of the tribes was smaller: a few votes were enough to shift enough tribes and reorient the Tributa against the Senate and the optimates in general. The equestrians could spook the Senate at will, and had won for themselves important concessions, such as sitting on trial juries for criminal and civil cases, something the optimates considered their exclusive privilege (no such right was extended to the populares, outside of the equestrians). Politically, the equestrians mostly supported the party of the populares, but they were ready to join the optimates' ranks once they had achieved a particular goal or privilege. This is not meant to disparage them: these were capable men, entrepreneurs who were able to pull themselves up by their own sandal straps. Their political ambitions did no more than reflect the nature of the rigid society they were born into. As equestrians, they could hope to mingle with the optimates and possibly—if their finances were large and generous enough— even join the Senate. This happened in very few cases, but the hope was there.

As Rome grew in wealth and power, it attracted a group of people who had no aristocratic lineage but neither were they poor. We can think of them as coming from the provincial middle class. They had land and slaves back home in the village of their birth, so they could live on their income. They often sold their services as lawyers or other professionals. The richer ones followed the equites' example and lent money at interest. The Romans viewed them with some contempt—their speech and manners were those of peasants— and called them *homines novi* (the new men). These new men came in all forms. Some were Roman citizens from nearby villages and were already part of the Tributa. Others were Roman citizens from allied towns but were not part of a tribe and so could not vote. Others were not Roman citizens at all, though if they were wealthy enough, some indebted politician might finagle a tribe for them. Politically, the new men tended to support the populares, whose paramount leader in Catiline's time was Gaius Marius, himself a new man. And the eagles of Marius's legions, the standards that had led the legions to the slaughter against the Teutones, Cymbri, and other tribes, became in effect the symbol of the populares. For years, the eagles sat secretly in somebody's house, possibly as a war trophy. When at last they emerged, they were in Catiline's hands, though by then Catiline was a very different man.

Two more points of the Roman political system matter in our story. The first is that while Rome had a public prosecutor's office (staffed by the two consuls, who were elected yearly, so this was a political task), the prosecutor could not on his own start a lawsuit against a Roman citizen except in cases of exceptionally serious crimes, like the murder of a family member or crimes against the state. Otherwise, the public prosecutor had to wait for a private citizen to file a lawsuit; then he could take over the legal matters. But we must remember that these were in the end political functions.

The second point relates to legal terminology. Each law was known by the name of the person who had introduced it in the Comitia. Thus, the Lex Valeria was a law introduced by Lucius Valerius Flaccus. The gens name of the sponsor of the law ("Valerius" means "one of the gens Valeria") used to identify the law had to be turned into feminine ("Valeria") because the noun "law" was feminine. Three laws matter in our story, the Lex Julia, the Lex Valeria, and the Lex Servilia, and we will refer to them by their Latin names.

3

CATILINE, SOLDIER

THE TALL, PALE TEENAGER WHO WALKED INTO THE army recruitment office in 90 BC was the son of Lucius Sergius Silo and Belliena. The gens Sergia had played an important role in Rome's early history: its members had filled many offices over the centuries, including praetor, consul, and *pontifex maximus* (religious leader). But no new office had come their way in the recent past and the family fortunes had shrunk, since that was how you replenished your coffers. Catiline's mother, Belliena, also came from a noble family, and her brother, Lucius Bellienus, was linked to a group of optimates who, throughout Catiline's youth, plotted to reverse the reforms of the last few years, possibly even to get rid of Marius altogether.

According to the historian Sallust (86–35 BC), who knew Catiline, the last of the Sergii "had a powerful intellect and great physical strength. . . . He could endure hunger, cold and lack of sleep to an incredible degree. His mind was daring, shrewd and versatile . . . [he was] an excellent speaker." That sounds like a pretty good recruit—if it was not for the rest of the description: Sallust says that Catiline had "an evil and depraved nature. Civil war, murder, rapine, and civil discord were gratifying to this young man from a very early age and he spent his youth carrying them out. . . . Longing for others' things, he excelled in greed . . . his wasted, incredibly immoderate mind was always after some great thing." After this description there followed a list of accusations (lewdness, corruption, profligacy, murder) that have marked the story of Catiline ever since. In effect, Sallust branded him as a criminal psychopath. He had political reasons to describe Catiline in these terms, and likely a few personal ones, as we shall see. Besides, Sallust was one of the new men, while Catiline was a descendant of one of Rome's oldest families. Throwing mud on haughty adversaries has always made political sense: some of the mud always sticks. In Catiline's case, so much stuck that he was unrecognizable for centuries afterward.

Catiline was enrolled in the legions commanded by Pompeius Strabo, who had been elected consul for that year. We do not know Catiline's rank, but out of deference to his family, he is likely to have been higher up than a simple soldier, possibly a junior officer. The task before Strabo's army was to move against the Italic allies who were fighting Rome over the citizenship issue.

Strabo proved a capable military commander, repeatedly defeating the former allies. We do not know how Catiline fared in his first war. We do know that among the other junior officers was Strabo's son, Gnaeus Pompeius Magnus, known to history as Pompey the Great, or simply Pompey. Years later, Pompey married Julius Caesar's daughter and, together with Crassus (who by then had defeated Spartacus) and Caesar himself, formed the three-men triumvirate (*triumviratus*) that ended any pretense of democracy in Rome.

But that was twenty years in the future. As Catiline saw action under Strabo's command in the Italic campaign, the other consul, Lucius Porcius Cato, was defeated and killed by the former allies. This might have made Rome's position difficult if Strabo hadn't scored victory after victory. Side by side with Strabo's successes, a younger officer named Lucius Cornelius Sulla mounted an offensive and defeated the army of the Samnites, tough mountain troops who had given Rome a great deal of trouble in the past. Another Roman general we have met, Gaius Marius, called out of a sort of self-imposed retirement after the murders of Saturninus and Glaucia, also won important engagements, so that by 88 BC, the war with the Italic peoples was effectively over.

The immediate military threat had ceased, but the war had put a massive strain on Rome: the Italic armies were made up of soldiers who knew Roman tactics and formations—in fact, they probably knew the Roman generals fighting against them one by one—and almost certainly many of them fought using Roman weapons (as Spartacus had done). The usual advantages of the Romans had dwindled, and the war dragged on far longer than it might have against a different enemy. Furthermore, the Italic troops usually made up the bulk of the Roman army, but now they fought against it. Rome itself, and the few cities that had remained loyal, supplied only a small proportion of the fighting force. Exceptional generals like Strabo, Sulla, and Marius managed to offset these handicaps, and the Romans' strict command-and-control discipline probably made a big difference. But the war had been a close call. And unlike the situation after other wars, it was not possible to waste the defeated enemy's land and cities: Rome needed them to be up and running soon, to reconstitute the army and march off to deal with another big threat that was materializing in the east. Politically, the Italic allies' demands had to be satisfied in some way. That way was the Lex Julia (Julian Law).

The Julian Law was quickly passed. It gave full Roman citizenship to all communities that had not fought in the civil war. To communities—note—not to individuals. Each community had to pass the law, accepting it as a whole, for it to apply to its citizens. Only then would the Senate attach any given community to an existing tribe in the Comitia Tributa, where it would count as one vote among many. And members of that community would thereby become Roman citizens.

The effect on the Roman political equilibrium was likely to be close to zero, so for many years before further reforms were carried out, Italic discontent remained. But the people were less angry than they had been, because the sheer fact of Roman citizenship provided some important protections. A supplementary statute allowed inhabitants of rebellious towns disqualified by the Lex Julia to apply for citizenship on an individual basis. Again, it was a matter of finding the right tribe to put these eager new men into.

Returning to Rome, the young Catiline, now a veteran of one civil war, was attached to the army commanded by the new consul, Sulla. The new commander belonged to the gens Cornelia, which had given Rome some of its most remarkable generals. Among them was Publius Cornelius Scipio, who had defeated Rome's worst enemy, Hannibal, at the battle of Zama on October 19, 202 BC, and had in effect brought Carthage under Roman supremacy. As with Catiline's family, we are talking about the flower of Roman aristocracy. And as with Catiline's family, Sulla's branch of the gens Cornelia had fallen on hard times. But at least it now had a consul and a glorious general. Its fortunes were bound to rise.

Catiline was still very young, twenty, when he was attached to Sulla's legions, and it isn't difficult to imagine how important the older man's example was for him. When Catiline returned to Rome from serving under Strabo, Sulla was fifty. He had climbed up the greasy pole of the cursus honorum all the way to the top. In a couple of years he would likely be assigned a nice, fat province to govern, and then the fortunes of his branch of the gens Cornelia would pick up again, returning its members to the position that by antiquity and previous glory was rightfully theirs. Nobody could have failed to see the parallel: it was up to Catiline to follow in his general's footsteps and restore the prestige and fortunes of the gens Sergia.

Interestingly, there was an important link between Catiline and his commander: Sulla had organized meetings of disgruntled aristocrats during Marius's dictatorship and also during the years that had followed, when the old perennial consul's men in effect lorded it over the city. Among the people who apparently regularly took part in these meetings was Lucius Bellienus, Catiline's uncle. We have no evidence that Catiline also attended, but since he was a minor, it seems unlikely. But Bellienus's presence in Sulla's home reveals the atmosphere in which Catiline grew up: one of aristocratic nostalgia for the days when the old Roman morality dictated the politics of the city, rather than the spreading vulgarity of the new men and their hired thugs. In that past age there was law, respect, devotion to the republic, and self-sacrifice. The currency of prestige was glory and personal accomplishment, especially in battle and in government. Whatever else, it was not gold. There was unity of purpose, harmony among the classes, and all of the ancient virtues thanks to which Rome had broken peoples much more numerous than itself and had set out its laws to everybody's benefit. Nowadays any ignorant peasant with lands seized from honest workers or, worse still, from an aristocrat, could command enough votes to have himself elected to the sacred offices of the city and trample better people than he.

We do not know whether Sulla's meetings were just exercises in venting aristocratic frustration or there actually were operational plans to oppose Marius and his gangsters. In any event, the meetings probably stopped when Sulla was called to fight the Italic rebellion. But if Bellienus was there, he likely discussed what was said in Sulla's home with his sister, Catiline's mother, and her husband, Sergius Silo. Even if Catiline was still a minor and not admitted to the dining area, he was probably within earshot. It is not difficult to imagine what this tall, brooding adolescent made of these accounts, when he could see the poverty in which his family lived while fat, worthless men ruled Rome. When in a few years his turn came to fight, he fought with a vengeance. And he kept doing that for the rest of his life.

Shortly after the end of the Italic civil war, Sulla, with Catiline among his staff, was given a new assignment: defeat that pesky King Mithridates. With a newly trained army, Sulla left Rome in 88 BC.

Mithridates had started out as king of a small portion of northern Anatolia, in what is modern-day Turkey. He had managed to expand his kingdom by defeating local rulers so that eventually his possessions extended from Armenia to the straights that separate Asia from Europe. This not only blocked access to the Black Sea (the Romans called it the Pontus Euxynos, hence Mithridates's title, "king of the Pontus"), but posed a threat to Rome's possessions in Greece. For a while Rome could do nothing about it: it had only a few legions in the area as it fought with the Italic allies. The peace was uneasy, as any peace must be between two forces that know they will eventually fight each other. But while the Italic populations were rebelling, all Rome could do was try to keep Mithridates sweet, avoid any-thing that smacked of provocation, and generally smile, one presumes through tightly gritted teeth. As soon as the Lex Julia settled the citizenship question, however, the Senate decided it had smiled long enough and sent Sulla out to fight Mithridates.

Before that, however, a strange event took place in Rome, an event with far-reaching consequences: a trib-une elected for the year 88 BC, Publius Sulpicius Rufus, introduced a motion to transfer the command of the coming expedition from Sulla to Marius. Rufus may have taken this utterly brainless initiative to make sure the old leader of the populares would support some political measure that was dear to his heart, but Marius—who must have been consulted—ought to have known better. In any event, neither seems to have realized that trying to pull the rug out from under Sulla's feet was somewhat unwise while Sulla had command of six legions, all of them not far from Rome. That meant thirty thousand men, fully armed and ready to fight. On receiving the news of Rufus's motion, Sulla simply turned his legions around and marched on Rome, in effect besieging it.

This was the first time a Roman general had reached the city with his full army. Soon it was to become a habit. At the last minute, Marius organized a corps of gladiators to repel Sulla and promised freedom to the slaves who would fight for him against the threat from the consul's army. This did not help: Sulla's veterans quickly routed the gladiators and killed Rufus. Hardly any slaves had been foolish enough to accept Marius's offer, knowing the kind of death that awaited them at Sulla's hands. Marius managed to slip through the legionaries' fingers and ran away to the African provinces. Sulla remained in Rome for a few months; there he supervised a good massacre of Marius's supporters and undid many of Marius's political reforms (though not his military reorganization), thereby restoring the power of the Senate. At last he left with his legions for the war against Mithridates.

This episode matters a great deal because it showed that a clearheaded man in charge of a military force could suspend any law passed in Rome and enforce his own will. The Senate was too cowed after years of Marius's control to take any measures to restore the rule of law and would acquiesce to anything that protected its own privileges. Without the leadership of the new men and their followers, the poor of Rome would not take part in a violent struggle to improve their economic and political standing. Most importantly, Sulla was able to blame Marius and his lot for everything that had gone wrong in Rome. These were dangerous lessons to learn, and Sulla left for the war against Mithridates with his head full of them. He would put them in practice in the future.

On his staff for this new war were a number of brilliant young officers: Cornelius Dolabella, Lucius Licinius Lucullus, and, most importantly, Antonius Hybrida. Each of them was to play a role in Catiline's tragedy. They had all taken part in the Italic wars, and with their general were now on their way to rid Rome of the threat from the east.

The war against Mithridates lasted years; fighting raged up and down the rugged terrain of Anatolia. Sulla commanded the Roman troops in the first phase, defeating two of Mithridates's armies in 86 BC. After his second victory, he probably could have pressed his advantage and won, but there were new problems in Rome. Sulla had to return home to settle his scores with Marius's supporters, so he agreed to much easier peace conditions for Mithridates than he probably could have imposed. The result was that about a decade later, war flared up again and was fought by Lucullus (74–67 BC).

Lucullus eventually managed to corner Mithridates and was ready for a final battle. But just then equites-sponsored intrigues in Rome caused him to be recalled. Lucullus was an old-style aristocrat who despised the financial shenanigans of the equites and had introduced several measures to limit their activities in the Pontus. This had enraged the financial élite in Rome, and since virtually all politicians were in their debt, it had not been difficult to apply political pressure to obtain the recall of this impudent general. Once Lucullus left to return to Italia, his position was handed over to Strabo's son, Gnaeus Pompeius Magnus, who got the credit for finally defeating Mithridates. This victory of Pompey's proved an important stepping-stone to his eventual participation in Crassus's and Caesar's dictatorship.

Shortly after Sulla left the war operations in 85 BC, a leader of the populares, Lucius Cornelius Cinna (from the same gens as Sulla, but a different branch) got the Senate to appoint him consul—appoint, not elect, in violation of the laws of the republic. Using the same tactics as Marius had, Cinna took advantage of Sulla's absence from Rome to get himself reappointed in 86, 85, and 84 BC. In effect, his supporters occupied the city, like Marius's had twenty years earlier. Nobody was willing to fight them, so over and over again, Cinna was appointed consul of the republic. And right by Cinna's side was none other than the old warhorse himself, Gaius Marius, returned from his refuge in Africa.

For a while Cinna's mob simply overran the city, beating people up and intimidating and generally shouting down any potential competitor. This created the ideal conditions for Marius to orchestrate a steaming bloodbath. He directed his followers to kill Sulla's supporters, friends of his supporters, people suspected of being friends of his supporters, and so on in an endless purge. Hundreds, maybe thousands, were slaughtered, without trial, in the streets and in the squares. The Senate, the ultimate guarantor of legality in Rome, spooked, was silent. The butchery was so long and terrifying that eventually Cinna himself called on the few military units that were stationed in Rome and set them against the populares murderers. This restored a peace, of sorts, in the city. Political murder became a bit more difficult. The soldiers imposed a kind of respite because they were better armed and trained than Marius's and Cinna's mobs. However, Marius and Cinna now controlled Rome with soldiers who obeyed their orders—the two were the consuls of the republic, and therefore the commanders in chief, after all. Soon Marius and Cinna appointed themselves consuls for the following year.

Just then, Marius died.

He was not poisoned, stabbed, drowned in the Tiber, hit with roof tiles (as had happened, after Sulla's victory, to some of Marius's friends), or otherwise murdered. He was over seventy, rather past the age Roman men of his period could hope to live, and died of natural causes. If there had been the slightest suspicion of foul play, his mob would have returned to the streets and Rome would have gone up in smoke.

So Cinna ruled alone, with no constraint from the Senate or the Comitia, and for a while the situation was as quiet as could be expected.

In 84 BC, when he was still consul (illegal though his office was), Cinna tried to get Sulla out of the way. There was no doubt in his mind that as long as the general was alive, his own life hung by a thread. He took an army and crossed to Greece to attack Sulla, who was still on his way back to Rome from Anatolia. But for reasons that are not entirely clear to us today, Cinna's soldiers revolted and murdered him in Greece. It may have been that many of them were Sulla's veterans and therefore unwilling to fight their old commander. We do not know.

With Cinna's death, there was nothing between Sulla and the walls of Rome. And that was where he aimed.

In spring 83 BC, Sulla landed in Italia from Greece, and his twenty-five thousand men were reinforced by troops led by Crassus, Caecilius Metellus Pius, and Gnaeus Pompeius Magnus. By the standards of the times, this was a reasonably sized army, and more importantly, it consisted entirely of battle-hardened veterans. Not someone you'd want to meet in an open field unless you had overwhelming numerical superiority. Nobody had that superiority in Italy.

Sulla marched slowly up the Italian peninsula, deliberately looking for and wiping out armies sent by Marius's supporters in Rome. There was something calculated and cold-minded about his progress: he meant to finish off the populares once and for all. While he was marching up from the south, Sulla sent detachments to fight units of populares well to the north, for example, besieging and eventually burning the town of Clusium in Etruria (today's Chiusi in Tuscany, 105 miles north of Rome).

True to his mission, he took no prisoners.

After a slow and systematic march, Sulla eventually laid siege to Rome (it was becoming a habit with him) and met the main body of the populares just outside the Collina Gate on the northeastern edge of Rome's walls, in October 82 BC. Sulla's troops attacked the defensive lines, and the battle lasted all day and all night. The accounts speak of tens of thousands dead.

These figures may be exaggerated, but remember the conditions under which Roman soldiers fought: wearing heavy armor, carrying javelin and sword, pushing with their (heavy) shields against their adversary, stabbing almost blindly into the opposing lines, even very fit men could probably not last in active combat longer than fifteen minutes or so. The physical demands were intense, and the psychological stress of possibly being wounded or killed made the effort even more challenging.*

Someone had understood that there had to be a continuous replacement of the frontline troops, a replacement that had to be seamless so the other side could not take advantage of it. That someone had been Marius, and his military reforms introduced the training necessary to have soldiers interchange their roles without stopping the fighting. But it took hundreds of hours to hone the average legionary into performing this maneuver, just as seventeen centuries later it took months of training to teach British troops to form their lethal "squares." Nobody who had not undergone that training could improvise the maneuver.

Thus a well-trained and experienced Roman army (like Sulla's) was in a position to deliver a consistently high level of violence for hours, possibly days. Its opponent, unless equally well trained, would be able to respond for a limited time, but as the legionaries traded places and new ranks came forward, the psychological

---

*A clear analysis of what fighting was like for Roman legionaries is in John Keegan, *A History of Warfare* (Toronto: Key Porter, 1993), 235–298.

and physical strain would begin to tell on their opponents. Brave men would collapse, exhausted. Others would flee and hide, not because they gave up the struggle but because they were simply unable to sustain the necessary level of effort. At that point, a well-trained army could simply move out over the field and systematically slaughter its drained enemy. This was done quickly and efficiently: a legionary would thrust his sword, the gladius, into the space near the neck above the top left rib of the collapsed fighter, severing the cardiac artery and causing immediate death. Which was preferable to the alternatives (including crucifixion and fighting to the death in the arena).

Under these circumstances, armies that were equally trained and experienced would probably leave relatively few dead on the field, and the bigger force would in general win the day. But if there was a significant difference between the combatants in training and abilities, the collapse of a legion's opponents was pretty well assured, and then the wholesale killing would begin. That seems to have happened at the Collina Gate.

Sulla's well-trained army faced a much larger force. But it was a disorganized army, a force of populares banded together to fight off the return of a hated general whose political intentions were already clear. These people fought with the courage of desperation and at some point managed to pin the center of Sulla's army against the city walls. For a moment things looked dim for Sulla, but the commander of his right wing was able to unleash a murderous assault against the populares, break through, and allow Sulla's force to spread out again. That commander was Catiline.

After this, the populares were routed and killed as they ran or lay on the ground prostrate with fatigue. In the end, Sulla's troops captured about three thousand of them.

But there was to be no pity. The victorious Sulla had them dragged in front of the army recruitment office in the city center and, in a horrific day, had them all killed in various gruesome ways. He was imparting a lesson and felt that gory deaths were the best way to make his point.

With the battle at the Collina Gate, Sulla became the master of the city. And the slaughter began again. The terrified Senate, on his instructions, voted the Lex Valeria, by which he was appointed dictator for life, in violation of the constitution: the dictator could only be appointed for six months at a time in moments of national emergency; the last had been during Hannibal's approach to Rome over a century earlier.*

There is no doubt that in Sulla's mind, Marius, Cinna, and the others had constituted a national emergency of the most severe type, worse even than the Italic rebellion

---

*It was called "Valeria" from the name of the president of the Comitia Centuriata, Lucius Valerius Flaccus. He introduced it and got it passed in 82 BC. Because nobody vetoed it, it became the law of the republic. Valerius Flaccus had been consul with Gaius Marius in 100 BC and had attempted to bring about a reconciliation between populares and optimates, without success. After some supporters of Cinna's killed members of Valerius Flaccus's gens, he pulled closer to Sulla. The political and legal background to the law are discussed in Frederik Juliaan Vervaet, "The 'Lex Valeria' and Sulla's Empowerment as Dictator (82–79 BC)," *Cahiers de l'Institut Gustave Glotz* 15 (2004): 37–84.

of the previous years. The traitorous allies could be met in the open and defeated, as Sulla had repeatedly done, provided the republic stood firm and supplied the general in the field with the arms, the equipment, and the trained troops he needed. If the republic could not do that, if, in fact, it acted openly against the army general, trying to replace him in his position of command as Marius had attempted, then the republic was in danger.

The dictatorship, then, had to be extended to ensure that no such danger would ever arise again. And the dictator, the man whose command could be counted on to protect and rebuild the republic, could only be the man who had shown himself able to deal with foreign threats and internal treason. That man was Sulla, in whose hands rested the protection of the city. The government of Rome, the command of its military, the peaceful existence of society, all were conflated in him. Sulla *was* the state.

In this perspective, the massacre of the prisoners taken in battle at the Collina Gate was not an act of gratuitous cruelty: it was a carefully aimed measure to undo the damage done by Marius. Letting the prisoners live would have been cruel to the Romans: their presence among the people could only become a new threat to the city. The massacre was surgery, the removal of a sick portion of the body so the rest might prosper. The same motivation would arise twenty years later.

But Sulla could not be sure that the prisoners' slaughter would be enough to stop the illness. In fact, he could be sure it would not: one way or the other, too many people had collaborated with Marius, Cinna, and the rest. The contagion was still there, under the surface but ready to flare up again. So Sulla devised the next step.

He compiled lists of people who had supported Marius and Cinna, lists of friends of the people who had supported them, lists of people who knew the friends of the supporters, and so on. So far, Sulla was repeating what Marius had done earlier. But Sulla had a more lucid mind than Marius and added a new twist: he had the lists, known as proscription lists, written out and posted in the Forum. The people named on the lists would be executed. In fact, they were fair game to all—they could (should) simply be killed without any annoying official sentencing. Their property (which included slaves and landholdings) would be confiscated and sold at auction (curiously, most of these properties ended up in the hands of Sulla and his friends, making them immensely rich). If you sheltered or helped a proscribed individual, you were thereby proscribed yourself, and the same confiscation would apply to your property. Anyone killing someone on the list would be rewarded.

The posting of the proscription lists in the Forum was a novel and clever step. It ratcheted up the terror, making citizens each other's potential murderers. To understand how important the Forum was in Sulla's scheme, we must understand what the Forum meant to the Romans.

The word "forum" derives from a verb (*ferre*) meaning "to carry, to bring," which gives a hint of its original function: the Forum was a marketplace where goods were brought to be sold. It was a wide, flat area of ground stretching south from the Capitoline Hill, far enough from the Tiber to be safe from the annual floods but close enough to benefit from river transport. On the Capitoline Hill, the city's mythical founder, Romulus, had established the first settlement, and around the Forum over time, temples and official buildings had been raised. From the foot of the hill, at the edge of the Forum, began the roads that linked Rome's expanding empire: this was "mile 0," the symbolic heart of Roman power. In the Forum, you talked business and struck deals, discussed politics, reviewed your legal cases with your lawyer, listened to candidates' speeches, worshipped your gods and sacrificed to them, and cheered the victorious, returning legions.

But above all the Forum was a place of law: the fundamental law of the republic, written on twelve bronze tablets, had been posted—after the usual fights between optimates and populares—in the Forum around 450 BC. What exactly was on these tablets we do not know. We have reports by ancient authors about some fragments, and from that it seems that the twelve tablets were a series of definitions of private rights and procedures. The originals were destroyed when the Senones, a Gallic tribe from northeastern France that had moved into Cisalpine Gaul, sacked Rome in 390 BC, and the tablets were never replaced. By Sulla's time, over three centuries later, the memory of their contents must have been reasonably faint, but that did not matter: the tablets had in a sense consecrated the Forum as the place where the Senate and the people of Rome made their decisions public. This was the Place of the Law.

Posting the proscription lists in the Forum in effect meant putting them on the same level as the laws and statutes of the Senate and the Comitia. This was a qualitative jump: Marius had slaughtered people by the thousands, but that was recognized as a political act, a fight between opposing parties. On the contrary, the proscription lists were, in some way, official: since the Senate was too cowed to send someone to take them down, they became in practice official. The Roman state wanted you to go murder so-and-so, and not only would it not prosecute you, it would reward you. Go do it.

It was a bloodbath.

The Greek historian Plutarch, over 120 years later, wrote, "Sulla now began to make blood flow, and he filled the city with deaths." Ancient authors talk of one thousand five hundred optimates and equites put to death, and possibly eight thousand populares. One name that ended up on the proscription list was Julius Caesar's, who had lukewarmly backed Marius and the populares, largely because he was Cinna's son-in-law. But Caesar was also an aristocrat from a well-connected family, and many of his relatives had supported Sulla and were still working for him. While the nineteen-year-old Caesar quickly made himself scarce, in Rome his relatives got to work on the dictator, bent his ear with great enthusiasm, and eventually talked him into removing Caesar's name from the list. Writing almost 150 years later, the Roman historian Suetonius claimed that as Sulla scratched the name out, he grumbled that they would regret keeping this Caesar alive because he would be dangerous in the future.

In the fall of 43 BC, Caesar himself reintroduced proscription lists.

In the midst of the massacre, Sulla implemented his reform program: among other, less important measures, the Senate had to approve any bill before it could be submitted to any popular assembly. The role of the

Centuriata, the older, more aristocratic of the assemblies, was restored. Powers of the tribunes of the poor were sharply cut back, possibly in part in revenge for the fact that Sulla had been stripped of his command in the Pontus campaign through the underhanded activities of a tribune. Over the previous three hundred years, the tribunes had often challenged the optimates and attempted to deprive the aristocracy of power in favor of the populares. This nonsense would now stop.

His reforms also took away the tribunes' power to introduce legislation. Ex-tribunes could not hold another office, ever, so being elected tribune became a dead end and discouraged clever men from running for it. Also, the veto power of the tribunes was ended.

The number of magistrates elected in any given year was increased, and all newly elected quaestores automatically became members of the Senate. The Senate went from three hundred to six hundred members, which gave it a political weight it had not had in centuries. The Senate was also given back the control of the courts from the equites, undoing one of the Gracchus brothers' reforms.

Having seen how easy it was for a general backed by loyal legions to seize power, Sulla introduced rules to prevent it from happening again. He reintroduced the rule that any officers of the republic had to wait ten years before running for reelection and created a system whereby, after serving in Rome during their year in office, all consuls and praetores would be given a provincial army as a governor for the following year.

A year after seizing power, Sulla resigned his dictatorship. The lifetime appointment of the Lex Valeria had in practice lasted only twice as long as the regular dictator-ship. He sent his legions home and called consular elections. He even ran for the office of consul for the following year, 80 BC, and was elected with Quintus Caecilius Metellus Pius, a relative of his fourth wife, Caecilia, and victorious general in the war against Sertorius. To prove that the situation had settled down, Sulla dismissed his bodyguards and walked around in the Forum, encouraging people to come and debate with him so he could explain his actions as dictator. At the end of the year, Sulla withdrew to his country villa near Puteoli (today's Pozzuoli, near Naples). He died there in 78 BC.

The proscription lists made the reforms of 81 BC possible: nobody dared oppose the dictator as long as the killing went on or could be resumed at a moment's notice. Even after Sulla dismissed his legions and had the men settled on the fertile lands of Etruria, the lists could be opened up again, and the slaughter could resume.

And while the carnage had lasted, Sulla's most trust-ed officers were in the thick of it, organizing and commanding death squads. They were still in Rome, like an unspoken threat, even after Sulla's retirement and death. As things settled down, these men were still walking around the streets. Among them were Crassus and Catiline.

Catiline had gotten a bad reputation from his participation in the proscription massacres, and rightly so: it was legalized murder, after all. Which massacres he participated in exactly we do not know, but it was alleged that he had tortured and killed his own brother-in-law, Marcus Marius Gratidianus, whose sister was Catiline's first wife. Gratidianus was Marius's nephew, not a desirable connection in Sulla's years. He had been a tribune in 87 BC at the time of Cinna's plot against Sulla and had supported Marius's and Cinna's return to Rome. This certainly made him a prime target for proscription. According to the two sources that relate this lurid tale, Catiline enticed Gratidianus to a place on the north side of the Tiber where many rich families buried their dead. There he broke Gratidianus's arms and legs, gouged out his eyes, and bled him to death on a grave. Then he cut off the corpse's head and carried it halfway across Rome to deposit it at Sulla's feet.

There is enough material here to shoot a horror movie, but it would be wholly fictional, since the account is substantially not believable. This story was the first step in the construction of the figure of Catiline as the depraved monster. It popped up again and again when political expedience made it worth using, as we shall see.

Let's start with this consideration: the person who claimed that this horrific event had taken place did not actually write it down, even though he was a prolific author. He outlined the incident seventeen years after the alleged facts, in an election speech. This speech was given in 64 BC, when this man was running for the office of consul. And who was running against the author of this story? Someone named Lucius Sergius Catiline.

The techniques of political smear campaigns were well advanced in ancient Rome. Even so, the allegations went a bit far: it is possible that Catiline did kill Gratidianus during the days of the proscription lists, but the torture strains belief. It is clearly crafted to depict a political adversary as a bloodthirsty, depraved madman by exaggerating an action that had happened under very particular circumstances. Even the location, a burial ground, is symbolic.

But did Catiline murder Gratidianus, even without torturing him? Actually, that is not clear either. Another enemy of Catiline's, the historian Sallust, never refers to Catiline when he discusses the death of Gratidianus. In fact, he does not even hint that the murder was the work of Catiline. Sallust simply describes the execution, saying the victim's "life was drained out of him piece by piece, that is: first his legs and arms were broken, and his eyes gouged out." Later Roman historians and writers (authors of the caliber of Livy, Seneca, and Lucan) repeated the story, adding new gruesome details to the torture and mutilation. Nobody questioned it. The monster was born.

But Sallust does not involve Catiline in the death and dismemberment of Gratidianus, so where did that idea come from? It came from the man who linked Catiline to the murder in that campaign speech of 64 BC: Marcus Tullius Cicero, lawyer, politician, and inexhaustible author, a provincial member of the equestrian order with great political ambition. We will return to Cicero later. For the time being, it's important to stress that he wrote extensively and that not once in his writings does he record, or even just refer to, the speech where he supposedly accused Catiline of the torture and murder of Gratidianus, nearly two decades after the event. Yet Cicero was in the habit of quoting himself at great length—to be uncharitable, we could say he was in love with the sound of his own words—and this void is surprising to say the least. It may be that he did leave a written account, but if so, it has been lost, a nobody appears to have seen it.

Given Sallust's silence, Cicero's silence on such a serious matter needs to be probed. How do we know about the speech where the accusation was made? It turns out to have been related by someone named Quintus Asconius Pedianus, a grammarian mostly noted for having written morally uplifting summaries of other authors' work for use by his sons (the *Odyssey* without the sex and violence must be a barrel of laughs). Now, here is catch number one: Asconius claims to report a fragment of Cicero's speech about this crime, but the fragment he quotes does not contain either Gratidianus's name or Catiline's. Asconius simply states that those were respectively the victim and the executioner.

And here is the second catch: Asconius was born around 9 BC, that is, fifty-five years after the election speech where the nefarious deeds were supposedly described. At best, someone must have told him, and told him when he was old enough to understand. Let's say that was at age eighteen. That means seventy-three years had passed since the speech, without any recording equipment being available. The telling may have been somewhat distorted or inaccurate, to put it mildly. In any event, that someone could not have been Cicero himself: he had died (in Caesar's proscriptions) in 43 BC, almost thirty-five years before Asconius's birth and well over half a century before Asconius could have understood what the issue was (again assuming that to be around age eighteen).

So we have the construction of a depraved monster murdering his own brother-in-law on the basis of an account that does not mention him or his victim and that, if it ever did, was first uttered in a political speech directed against the supposed murderer as an opposing candidate. This speech was reported several decades later by someone who could not possibly have been present at the event.

This goes beyond hearsay. We've moved from political tragedy to farce.

But for Catiline it was a tragedy.

The accusation, which must have made the rounds of the gossipmongers in Rome, tarred him forever. Never mind that he was at some point (we shall see when) tried for Gratidianus's murder and acquitted. The smell of sulfur was on him.

4

AFTER SULLA

W HILE CATILINE WAS PROMENADING AROUND Rome with a chopped off head, or so the story goes, Crassus was commanding death squads and growing rich. He was among the first to bid for the properties of those killed because of the proscription lists. He was already rich, but Sulla's proscription made him fabulously wealthy. He relied on this wealth to finance the political career that took him, as we saw, to the very top of Roman power and financed other political careers, such as Julius Caesar's.

From what we can tell nowadays, the murderous brutality of Crassus was no different from Catiline's, or any other death squad commander in those days. The difference is that Crassus was never accused of wickedness, as Catiline was for his role in those days of blood and death. And here is a detail worth noting: Crassus grew wealthy on the spoils of murder, but nobody, not even his worst enemies, ever accused Catiline of doing the same. Why not?

The only credible answer is that Catiline did not use the property of the dead for his own advantage. He was carrying out a task for Sulla's reformation of the republic, perhaps an unpleasant task, but at any rate not a personal vendetta. He was killing coldly, because killing meant ridding the republic of those people who had betrayed the values of the old aristocracy, his aristocracy. Poor though he was, he did not loot. He appears to have been one of the very few of Sulla's officers who did not.

After Sulla's death, the reforms he had set up to restrict the power of the poor simply came undone, one by one. Most important from our point of view, the undoing affected three people we are following in very different ways: Catiline and Crassus found themselves in rather difficult circumstances, in a political sense. Pompey, on the other hand, proceeded with his political career. The fact is that Pompey, unlike Crassus and Catiline, had stayed well clear of the proscription massacres. He had been a supporter of Sulla's, but he had made sure his hands were squeaky clean. Untainted by those days of unspeakable horror, he remained a popular general and a promising politician. Crassus, on the other hand, had been the overall coordinator of the proscriptions and had directed them in such a way as to benefit his own patrimony. Crassus was generally disliked, and it was difficult for him to return to active politics while the memory of Sulla was so fresh.

Crassus could simply withdraw to look after his immense possessions in the Ager Campanus, the countryside around Naples. There, fed, cared for, and respected, he could simply wait until Rome was again ready to receive him. But Catiline had nowhere to go; he had to stay in Rome, show his face, and look for a way to support himself. The family could not do it for him because no property had come his way from the proscriptions. At the end of Rome's most serious civil war, in which thousands had died and huge landed properties had changed hands for a pittance, Catiline was as poor as he had been before.

He had little option: aristocrats did not work manually, and in any event, he had reached the age of thirty without any training in that direction. But in the year 78 BC, two optimates and former supporters of Sulla's were elected consuls: Quintus Lutatius Catulus and Marcus Aemilius Lepidus. Catulus in particular was a gentle soul who tried to downplay Sulla's massacres so as to rebuild the civic connections of a deeply wounded Rome. Catulus was also a childhood friend of Catiline's and would in future years play an important role in his life. For the time being, we can just point this out: according to contemporary gossip, when Marius was in power, Gratidianus had prosecuted and driven to suicide Catulus's father. If so, the claim that Gratidianus was tortured and killed at the tomb of the gens Lutatia has a kind of poetic justice built into it. We do not have evidence of whether the story about Gratidianus and Catulus's father was true, though we know that Gratidianus had been one of Marius's supporters, so the anecdote is not unlikely.

In some way, the election of Catulus and Lepidus as consuls may have demonstrated no more than an as-yet-undiminished fear of Sulla. Be that as it may, Catiline was that year elected quaestor and, thanks to Sulla's reforms of the Senate, become a senator himself. Just as Sulla was dying in Puteoli, Catiline saw the cursus honorum open up before him. It must have seemed to him that the task he had set for himself from his very early youth was within reach: the gens Sergia now had for the first time in three centuries a son whose foot rested on the lowest rung of the ladder of the offices of the republic, leading over time to the power and wealth that were the proper legacies of a family as ancient and as noble as theirs.

We should not snicker at this idea. We live in a relatively mobile society where the very notion that our ancestors would determine what we do seems somewhat ridiculous to say the least. But to the Romans—and to virtually all societies before the twentieth century— ancestors shaped and defined what people did and thought. With them came the idea of the family not as parents-and-two-children but as a collection of ways of life, a sense of what could and could not be done. It may have been a suffocating situation at times, but it held a surprising stability, a certainty we have now lost.

The point is that Catiline, in his thirtieth year, won an elected office. Not a very important one, but that would come. If he played his cards right, higher offices were within his reach as soon as his age allowed him. The new consuls, that is, the highest officers of the republic, came from the same political party and the same traumatic experience of the proscription lists put up by Sulla as he did, and they certainly protected him, or at least looked upon him with favor. He was no threat to them—too young to aim at high elected office—but if he was encouraged and pushed forward would provide a kind of safety barrier in a dozen years' time, when they might no longer be able to protect themselves.

At thirty years of age, Catiline was just over the minimum for the office. We know little about his year as quaestor. That, too, is significant: there were no accusations against him for the year 74 BC. He did not yet threaten anybody. As evidence of that, the following year he was sent as a representative of Rome to Macedonia, a reasonably important role that would suggest further promotion in future years, or if not promotion at least a successful political career. In fact, in 70 BC, Catiline was elected aedilis, and in 68 BC, praetor. This was an immensely important office, and Catiline reached it just as he turned the minimum age to be elected.

That Catiline climbed the ladder of public offices in ten years, picking them out one by one at the first opportunity, says something about his abilities as a campaigner and public speaker. He was obviously an attractive, possibly a charismatic candidate. His past as one of Sulla's henchmen does not seem to have held him back: he may have mellowed as he grew older and as he observed from close quarters the machinery of power. But however convincing he may have been in the political race, campaigns needed money, as they do now. So Catiline's success raises the question of the source of his finances. It certainly was not his own purse, given what we know of his circumstances. We have no direct evidence of this, but there seems to be no reason to doubt who paid Catiline's bills: Crassus.

And not just Catiline's: the richest man in Rome was also betting on another ambitious young man, Julius

Caesar, who owed Crassus some 25 million sestertii. This was no small matter: since Tacitus says that a legionnaire's annual salary after Marius's reforms was 900 sestertii, Caesar's debt was enough to pay twenty-eight thousand men—that is, five legions—for a year. And Caesar was only one of the political wannabes indebted to Crassus. No wonder Crassus was nicknamed *dives* ("the rich man").

Crassus was following a clear political strategy: by financing former supporters of both Marius's (Caesar) and Sulla's (Catiline), he was spreading his political assets and protecting himself, whatever may happen. Helping those who had fought for Marius, he was also building up goodwill with the populares, something that mattered a great deal to a former Sulla man like himself. So, shortly after the death of the dictator, it was politics as usual in Rome: senators, equites and populares were bickering over the makeup of juries, over the powers of the tribunes, over land reform and debt reduction.

But starting in the mid-70s BC, three foreign crises and one domestic problem came to spice up the routine of Roman politics.

The first crisis was a leftover from Marius's days and involved a very able Roman general named Quintus Sertorius in Spain. Sertorius had sided with Cinna and Marius, though he was disgusted by their political massacres. As Sulla marched on Rome in 82 BC, Sertorius, who that year was the governor of Spain, stayed put, and in 78 BC began a campaign of personal conquest of that province. He was a leader who knew how to motivate his men and soon won the admiration and loyalty of the local population, even though the Roman citizens living there did not recognize his authority. Sertorius, backed by local warriors and some faithful legions, again and again defeated the generals sent from Rome to re-conquer Spain: Quintus Caecilius Metellus Pius and Pompey himself. This war went on for six years, leading to a considerable drainage of military forces for Rome. In 74–73 BC, Sertorius's army lost some engagements with Metellus and Pompey, and in 72 BC, Sertorius was assassinated by his officers, who were losing faith in his command abilities. Arriving home, Pompey received yet another nice procession through the streets of Rome—much to Crassus's annoyance, one imagines.

Meanwhile there was trouble on the other end of the empire: the old fox, Mithridates, went on the prowl again. Already as Sulla was busy slaughtering his fellow citizens, Mithridates had launched a new war against Rome (83–81 BC). He scored some important victories but realized he did not have the strength to drive the Romans out of Anatolia, so he settled for a peace treaty and immediately started preparing a new army. In 73 BC, he attacked the Romans again, starting a war that was to last ten years. The Senate sent back Lucius Licinius Lucullus, a close ally of Sulla's and reckoned at the time to be the best general Rome had. Lucullus beat Mithridates in engagement after engagement and pursued him into neighboring Armenia, where he razed the capital. All these victories notwithstanding, he did not manage to capture Mithridates. At this point (66 BC) the Senate, tired of waiting, sent Pompey. Mithridates gave him the slip, too, and tried to persuade one of his sons to raise yet another army against the Romans for a campaign in 63 BC. When the son refused, Mithridates had him killed and went to talk to a second son, who refused to help and actually joined forces with the Romans. That was when Mithridates committed suicide, bringing the war to a close. Again, Pompey took the credit.

Back in Rome, Lucullus, embittered by what he saw as the ungratefulness of his countrymen, retired to his villa on Mount Tusculum, about twelve miles south of the city, where he devoted his time to the study of cooking and Greek philosophy and literature. He died in 56 BC.

As if Sertorius and Mithridates weren't enough to deal with, the Senate kept hearing complaints of merchants and ship owners whose vessels were being ransacked by the pirates who hid out among the Greek islands and the coast of Anatolia. Some had even raided the coasts of southern Italy. Marcus Antonius (father of Caesar's friend Mark Antony) was appointed to deal with the pirates, which he did less than brilliantly. The war against piracy lasted decades and picked up again from time to time as Rome was more or less distracted by other events.

In 73 BC, the same year that Mithridates came back to fight his third war, the internal situation in Italia took a dramatic turn for the worse. About seventy gladiators managed to escape from a training school near Capua (north of Naples), defeat the local police detachment sent after them, and attract numerous recruits. Led by the gladiator from Thracia (modern Bulgaria) Spartacus, soon they were living off the land, stealing, murdering, and raising ever more slaves to fight with them. At first the authorities in Rome saw this as a policing issue, and it was only when the number of rebels swelled beyond all expectation that the Senate woke up and decided to send someone to teach these slaves a lesson. But with all the generals away from Rome in one war or another, it was difficult to find both the commander and the men to throw against the rebels.

Fortunately for Roman slave owners, a landlord with huge properties near where Spartacus was devastating the countryside offered to invest his own money to raise an army and hunt down the slaves. In 72 BC the Senate accepted, and Marcus Licinius Crassus got to work, raised an army, trained it, and left Rome to attack Spartacus. The following year the slaves were beaten; Spartacus died in the battle, and six thousand prisoners were crucified along the Appian Way as a reminder that a similar escapade would be distinctly unhealthy. To Crassus's renewed annoyance, Pompey, just returning from Spain, joined him in rounding up the escaped slaves, so that as they rode into Rome, Pompey's renown rose, and Crassus, who had spent his own money on the victorious army, did not shine as brightly as he had hoped.

From the Senate's point of view, this was a blessing. Grateful though they were to Crassus, the senators were even happier that both he and Pompey were now in Rome with their respective armies. Unlike the time of Sulla, when only one military force threatened the republic, there now were two, roughly balanced in numbers and experience. If one of the two generals moved against the city, the other would be at his throat in a matter of seconds. Crassus and Pompey understood that, too, so they ran together for the two offices of consul, full of praise for each other but with their armies within easy calling distance. And they got the jobs.

Pompey got his job even though he was only thirty-six, six years short of the minimum age. He advanced a number of reasonable arguments that would encourage the Senate to make an exception and let him be elected consul: he had beaten Sertorius, he had mopped up Spartacus's rebels, and his legions were a day's march from Rome. The Senate was very impressed by the last point especially.

The 70s BC ended on that note. Crassus and Pompey had been elected consuls in large part because their armies were near the city—which was exactly what Sulla had tried to prevent ever happening again. Neither one had a real political program outside of distributing land to his military veterans (Pompey) and replenishing their finances (both). They started their year as consuls by expelling from the Senate sixty-four men considered "unworthy" (out of three hundred, since Sulla's reform of the Senate had already been reversed). The concept of being unworthy was reasonably elastic for the Romans: it could cover corruption for financial gain, abuse of power in one form or another, sexual misbehavior, and generally bringing into disrepute the institution for which one was acting. Unworthiness was not written in the laws and defined as a certain type of behavior; it was a matter of general opinion: if enough people thought you were unworthy, then you were.

In 70 BC, Catiline was a senator. Three years earlier, he had been found not guilty of a serious crime. Our source for this is none other than Asconius, the man who, writing almost a century later, attributed to Catiline the torture and murder of Gratidianus.

What serious crime are we talking about? In 73 BC, Catiline was alleged to have had sexual relations with a vestal virgin. If true, this was serious: the vestals were handpicked young women who devoted their lives to the goddess Vesta, who symbolized harmony and the sacred hearth of Rome. They had to be virgins because that represented the purity of their tasks, to keep alive the sacred fire and to sacrifice daily. They embodied Rome as a concept, almost a family. Loss of virginity polluted the women and opened the city to Vesta's displeasure, with unknowable consequence. Seducing a vestal was a crime against the city, and punishment was severe. If found guilty, the woman was buried alive in a specially constructed mound near the Collina Gate. The man would be taken to the Forum and whipped to death. Actually, by Catiline's time, this punishment rarely took place, but it was still exercised on some occasions.

In a sense, more than the act itself, what mattered in this case was who the vestal was. Her name was Fabia, and she was the sister of Terentia, Cicero's wife. Asconius, who relates this story, draws this information from a passage of Cicero's campaign speech for the voting in 64 BC, in which he attacked his fellow candidate Catiline. Fabia was acquitted, and so was Catiline. But there was gossip that Catiline got off thanks to the influence of Quintus Lutatius Catulus, the man on whose family tomb Gratidianus's murder had taken place. Catulus was involved in the trial as a member of the religious court that judged such matters. He was a leading aristocrat, close to Sulla's party though not to its most violent wing.

Together with Catiline and Fabia, there were two other defendants in the same trial: a vestal named Licinia, and none other than Crassus. They, too, got off. The whole vestal sex scandal turns out to have been a tempest in a teapot. This is not to say that the defendants did not commit the crimes they were charged with, or that Catulus did not help them. But in the reality of heavily politicized Roman courts, having a friendly judge was the only way to ensure being let off. What matters for us is that the memory of the trial remained and that Cicero pulled it out of his hat when it suited him to provide firepower against a dangerous opposing candidate.

The judicial exoneration of Catiline had been unequivocal enough that in 70 BC, Pompey's demand that some individuals be expelled from the Senate did not affect him. And even if this could be dismissed as a favor Crassus did for him, the fact remains that Crassus was hard-nosed enough that if Catiline had been really tainted and thus proved a real liability, he would have been dropped like a hot potato—or a hot stone, since the Romans did not have potatoes. The following year, Catiline ran for praetor and was elected, again not something that could have happened without Crassus's support, given what we know of Catiline's finances. And Crassus did not back losers or questionable candidates.

In 68 BC, things were reasonably quiet in the Italic territories. Conflicts (Mithridates) were under way elsewhere and were none of a praetor's concern unless called upon to intervene by the Senate. Catiline appears to have spent his time in Rome, dealing with civil administration and courts. His eyes were focused on the end of the year, when he would be given the governorship of a province.

This was the focus of his entire political career, the step-ping-stone that would put him in a position to rebuild his family fortunes and move on to the final prize of the consular office. He was thirty-nine.

Along the way, Catiline had picked up a wife (whose name we do not know, though she must have been Gratidiana since his brother-in-law was the famous Gratidianus) and a son. Both of them died young, and his political enemies would use these personal tragedies later in his career. Catiline married again, around 66 BC, to Aurelia Orestilla, daughter of a rich (though not noble) family who already had a daughter from her first marriage. She was, by all accounts, beautiful. He was impoverished and indebted, and had a very dubious political future. Yet Orestilla stood by him to his death.

At the end of his uneventful year as praetor, Catiline was given a province to administer for 67 BC: Africa. That sounds fabulous, but the reality is much less legendary. The Romans called "Africa" only what we call Tunisia, the stretch of coast that is closest to Sicily, where Carthage had stood. To the west, Algeria was known as Mauretania and Numidia. To the east were Libya and Egypt. Africa was a small stretch of sand and ruins with a few old Phoenician cities on the coast. As a province for Catiline's purposes, it left a lot to be desired. It was definitely better than some other places, like the Gaulish provinces in the Alps or parts of Illyria (modern Serbia, Bosnia, and Croatia), but it was not a rich place where you could make your fortune. Even the cities along the coast, though rich, did not help: they were not provinces but "allies" tied to Rome by treaties approved by the Senate, and they therefore governed themselves. For an ambitious governor, this was not good news. You couldn't tax them, and you couldn't harass them.

Catiline had to watch his step not only because of the special legal status of the allies but also because Rome had been rocked a few years earlier by a scandal resulting from the behavior of another provincial governor, Verres. This man—we do not know his full name—had so riled the population of Sicily by arbitrary taxation and general abuse of his office that he was sued and managed to escape from Rome just as his trial started. Verres's trial had a profound effect, at least for a while: misgoverned provinces had found a threat they could dangle on their tormentors. This may not have greatly improved the standards of Roman governorship, but at least it marked the possibility of retribution and the ruin of a political career. On the other side of the coin, the Verres shock had created a bit of a witch-hunt mood, so that it opened perfectly decent governors to unfounded accusations purely for political ends.

One more point needs to be stressed: the public prosecutor who went after Verres was Cicero.

5

Cicero

W<small>E MUST TAKE A CLOSER LOOK AT THIS MAN</small> Cicero, who has cropped up in our story several times. Marcus Tullius Cicero is a difficult individual to deal with, because he has shaped so many aspects of Western culture, yet in some ways he embodied all manner of undesirable characteristics. He remained an outstanding example for lawyers, politicians, and writers well into the twentieth century and set out the rules of political and public debate in a way that, whether people know it or not, we are still following. He and Catiline crossed metaphorical swords, for although intellectually enterprising, Cicero was a physical coward and Catiline was not. Above all else, Cicero is responsible for the image of Catiline we still have as the immoral and depraved corruptor of people.

Cicero was born January 3, 106 BC, in a small hill town called Arpinum (today's Arpino) about sixty miles southeast of Rome. The town had been granted Roman citizenship in 188 BC, so it was not besieged or sacked by the Romans during the civil war. Though technically Roman, Cicero was in fact a provincial "new man" without connections to the senatorial class. The only possible link was a distant family relation to Gaius Marius, himself born in Arpinum, but that was not a desirable connection to advertise in his life. His family were reasonably well-off landowners belonging to the provincial middle class, the equites. According to Plutarch, who wrote his biography, the cognomen "Cicero" apparently derived from an ancestor who had a facial growth in the shape of a chickpea (*cicer* in Latin).*

In any event, Cicero was a sickly child who had trouble breathing, so he spent his time at home reading. While still young, he became well known for his learning and his skill at writing; apparently at age ten he wrote a longish poem that has been lost. As an adolescent he learned Greek and spoke it fluently, and was soon translating Greek philosophical and poetic works into Latin. His knowledge of Greek soon made him a desirable resource for the Roman aristocracy, which felt the need, as its empire expanded, to bring home to its successful but still culturally backward city the splendor of older civilizations.

*This is the standard account, but I suspect the origin of the nickname was that the family had made money selling chickpeas in Rome. Chickpeas (*cicer arietinum*) grow well in the hills of Arpinum and were one of the staples of the Roman poor.

In his midteens, Cicero moved to Rome, where he studied law with the man who was considered the foremost legal scholar of his time, Quintus Mucius Scaevola. In 88 BC, Scaevola defended Gaius Marius from Sulla's attempt to have his rival declared an "enemy of the people of Rome." Scaevola's cousins included Crassus.

To emphasize these connections, we are talking yet again about the pinnacle of Roman society, into which Cicero gained admittance in spite of his provincial origins and his link to Marius. Admittance but not membership: he was a provincial equestrian, and such he remained. To the sickly boy who had not passed his army admission exam, this hurt. He spent his life trying to show he was more senatorial than the senators, more Roman than the Romans.

He became a lawyer, and at that time, just as today, every lawyer needed a big case to make his name. Cicero's arrived in 80 BC, when he was twenty-six. A man closely allied with the powerful gens Metella, Sextus Roscius, was charged with patricide, a horrendous crime under Roman law. Cicero took his case. Like many lawyers since, Cicero's strategy was to defend his client by pointing the finger at someone else. Taking this case was a brave step for Cicero; not only was patricide an appalling crime, but the person Cicero accused of the murder of Roscius's father was Lucius Cornelius Chrysogonus, a Greek freedman of Sulla's. Chrysogonus had bought, for a song, the property of the proscribed Sextus Roscius Amerinus, Sextus Roscius's father. Defending Roscius could have been perceived as an indirect attack against Sulla, and the dictator could have simply ordered Cicero's throat to be slit. But it speaks volumes about Sulla's mindset that he did not try to protect Chrysogonus. Cicero got Roscius acquitted, and his reputation was made: he had (indirectly) faced the most powerful man in Rome and had won the case.

But Cicero had had to swim between two powerful and opposite currents, Sulla and the Metelli. His reputation was made, but he still judged it opportune to put some distance between himself and Rome—or rather, himself and Sulla. In 79 BC he left on a cultural trip to Greece, returning only after Sulla had died. In Greece he worked with teachers such as the rhetorician Apollonius Molon of Rhodes (who also taught Caesar some years afterward). There is a parallel here with young Americans going to Oxford and Cambridge Universities to earn their spurs and acquire a patina of Old World respectability.

Cicero returned to Rome in 77 BC. Before leaving on his trip, he had married Terentia, sister of the vestal virgin Fabia. Terentia seems to have come from a family with no noble background, the Terentii Varrones. But they had money, which was what an aspiring politician needed. The marriage lasted thirty years, after which Cicero divorced Terentia and married a girl much younger than he was. That marriage did not last.

Even though Cicero's medical condition had kept him from fulfilling his military duty, he started on his political career. Greek rhetoric, with its insistence on long, convoluted sentences, made him a fascinating speaker to the still unsophisticated Romans. Like Catiline, Cicero was elected to each office as soon as he ran for it: he was quaestor in 76 BC (at age thirty), aedilis in 70 BC (at thirty-seven), and praetor in 66 BC (at forty). But unlike Catiline, he rose all the way to consul, in 63 BC.

The parallel between these two men, the impoverished aristocrat and the upstart lawyer, tells us a great
deal about Roman society. Other politicians had managed to have the minimum age rules suspended for themselves: it was merely a matter of knowing and being
friendly with important senators who would introduce
objections for specific cases and sway the noble congre-
gation in their favor. If you plodded through each office
just as your age admitted you to it, you had to be either
a new man or a political loner—at any rate, someone
who could not draw on the support of powerful friends
and family. That both Cicero and Catiline were in this
position reveals the closed exclusiveness of Roman society and the corruption that derived from it. Perhaps
more importantly, it shows that political careers meant
subjecting oneself to the will of some powerful man or
other who could make or break you. Cicero, once back
from Greece and free from Sulla, decided to side with the
powers that would make him. Catiline, in the years that
followed his African adventure, increasingly defied the
established order. That was when he ran afoul of Cicero,
who had become the very embodiment of the established
order.

For Cicero, Roscius's acquittal had the effect of pushing him closer to the populares. But it was not by choice:
if you defeated a man of Sulla's entourage, you were necessarily one of the populares, or so it was thought. But it
could not last: Cicero, as the good member of the equites he was, saw the populares as dangerous, irreverent,
easily swayed by passion and not by reason. Like many
new men, he wanted to join the aristocracy, share their
privileges, be invited to their parties, deal with men of

ancient lineage on the same level. It was a hollow dream, of course, but it mattered to the sickly but bright provincial boy. He quickly pulled closer to the optimates. In 64 BC, he delivered four Greek-inspired speeches against the landownership reforms proposed by Servius Sulpicius Rufus, who was consul in 51 BC. We will come back to this attempted reform below. But at the time it was proposed, Cicero took the Senate's position and said no deal: the land belongs to the optimates, and that is all there is to it. The aristocracy loved him while at the same despising this weak, thin, provincial lawyer who defended their interests. They watched in complacent awe as he went a step farther. Under Sulla's proscription, the children and grandchildren of the people on the lists could not inherit the property of the deceased. Cicero argued in the Senate that to allow them to inherit was illegal. He even defended the equites' right to have a certain number of seat rows reserved for them at public plays. What more could a senator ask for?

Cicero became, in sum, an intransigent and blind reactionary, all the while defending his position under the guise of high moral ground: he consistently presented himself as a dignified, humanitarian, virtuous man motivated solely by the love of his country. The poor masses of Rome had, in his view, no legitimate claims: debts, loss of land, poverty were their own fault. And because he wrote and spoke well, for two thousand years intelligent people have believed him.

And he did write well. After his trip to Greece, his language became richer, more complex, and more expressive. He transformed Latin from a practical language suited to giving commands and describing the limited

reality of early Roman culture into a powerful intellectual language that held sway in the Western world for
twenty centuries and is still used in scientific work.
Reading his texts, one is impressed by the precision with
which he expresses his thoughts. He introduced into
Latin a number of words he translated from Greek, and
from Latin these spread throughout Western languages;
examples are *humanitas, qualitas,* and *quantitas.* It may
seem strange that such a reactionary man should be the
one to define the first of these terms, "humanitas," as the
virtues of an educated man necessary for a proper life of
public service. Reading literature, especially poetry, is the
hallmark of the man who has humanitas, said Cicero.
We still talk about "the humanities."

Without doubt, Cicero was an exceptional man in his
ability to deal with the language and bend it to his will.
He was also a vain man who rejoiced in twisting and
turning words so as to create complex and intertwined
sentences. Reading him, you feel he will never use one
word when three will do, and if he can find a complex
grammatical structure to replace a simple one, he will be
delighted to resort to it. Every conceivable, obscure
grammatical rule that could be connected to Latin, he
was only too happy to use. The result is that for twenty
centuries, his works have been used as a kind of Latin
paradigm for generations of school kids, giving them
stomachaches and an unreasonable hatred for the language. A protest ditty sung by British schoolchildren
about this went: "Latin's a dead language / as dead as it
can be / it's killed the ancient Romans / and now it's
killing me." No doubt they were referring to Cicero.

During his political career, Cicero clashed with
Catiline, and for years afterward, writes Plutarch, you

couldn't go to the Senate or a court audience without hearing Cicero going on about how he had saved Rome from the immoral and depraved Catiline. He started to get on people's nerves but did not seem to realize it. The provincial lawyer who had never been accepted by the aristocracy found in Catiline's conspiracy the proof that he, Cicero, was a real Roman. There is something terribly pathetic about this old man (old by the standards of the time) declaring that Rome had been reborn as a lucky city during his consulate.* He was not stupid, but his desire to fit in made him lose all sense of proportion.

After his consulate, Cicero twisted and turned in the political winds of the 50s BC. He sided at times with Caesar, at times with Pompey as the two of them fought for domination over the empire after Crassus was killed while invading Parthia (which overlapped parts of today's Syria and Iraq) in 53 BC. Neither really wanted him as an adviser, as he now marketed himself (did he, or did he not, have *humanitas* to spare?). After Caesar thrashed Pompey at the battle of Pharsalus (48 BC) and the old general had to escape to Egypt, Cicero did everything he could to gain Caesar's favor. To his disappointment, Cicero failed to win over Caesar's sympathy, but worse was in store. After Caesar was killed on March 15, 44 BC, Cicero pulled closer to Caesar's adopted son, Gaius Julius Caesar Octavianus, the future emperor of Rome under the name Augustus. Octavianus had no particular use for this old man and did not really attempt to protect him from political enemies. Mark Antony, who

*Cicero's own words were, "*O fortunatam natam me consule Romam!*" Plutarch, *Cicero*, 3.

was furious that Cicero had spoken publicly against him, accusing him of misusing Caesar's testament, sent out a troop of legionnaires and had Cicero killed as he was trying to escape, probably to Greece, on December 7, 43 BC.* According to some accounts, his head and hands were chopped off. His head, sent posthaste to Rome, was hung from one of the columns in the Forum that celebrated Rome's victory over Carthage a hundred years earlier. Someone stuck a big pin into the tongue of this macabre trophy, as if to remind his fellow citizens where Cicero's abilities had lain.

---

*Mark Antony (Latin: Marcus Antonius, 83–30 BC) was a general in the army and Julius Caesar's cousin. After having Cicero killed, he formed an alliance with the future emperor Augustus but soon fell out with him, bringing about a new civil war in which Mark Antony was defeated and killed himself together with his lover, Queen Cleopatra of Egypt. After this civil war, Rome was governed by the emperor, and the republic came to an end. In Shakespeare's tragedy *Julius Caesar,* the character inspired by Marcus Antonius delivers the famous speech that begins, "Friends, Romans, countrymen!"

6

CATILINE ON TRIAL

W E RETURN TO WHERE WE LEFT CATILINE AT AN important point in his life. In 67 BC, he arrived in Africa and discovered that the payback he was expecting was not going to happen. The province itself was sand, scrubland, and ruins. The cities of the coast, where the real money was, were Roman allies and therefore off-limits. If you moved into the interior, you just found more sand and the odd tribe of unfriendly desert nomads. Judging from what happened later, however, Catiline did his best. He found ways to gouge some money out of the locals, though we do not know exactly how he managed this. There is some suspicion that he arrived at an understanding with Jempsale, king of nearby Mauretania (modern Algeria and Morocco, not to be confused with today's Mauritania), concerning the application of a land-reform law that Catiline was thinking about, but we do not know any details. In any event, Catiline must have gotten something out of his year as governor because shortly after he came back to Rome in 66 BC, the residents of Africa sent the Senate a letter of complaint about him and declared their intention to pursue their former governor for bribery and corruption (*concussio*).

There has always been something vaguely surreal about this threatened lawsuit. In the first place, Catiline had just married (or was about to marry) a rich woman, Aurelia Orestilla: had he really needed to milk a bunch of poor Africans to finance his political ambitions? Granted, he was in debt to Crassus, but Crassus could wait and would call in his favors when he needed them. Catiline was bright enough to know this, and to know that repaying Crassus's loans did not necessarily involve handing over gold: political assistance was more likely to be required and accepted as a settlement. So why risk having lawsuits filed against him, and with them a disqualification from the candidacy for the long-sought office of consul? That was, after all, the step he needed to rebuild the fortunes of the gens Sergia, and to him this was an immensely important goal. We may have trouble understanding this driving desire of his, in these days of nuclear families with only minimal connections across generations. But at that moment in time, Catiline *was* the gens Sergia, the carrier of its glory, its name, its future. The Sergii had reached Italy's shore from Troy a thousand years before Catiline was born, and he intended to ensure they would last for another thousand. This was not cheap romanticism; it was a deeply felt sense of oneself as a link in a very long chain seamlessly intertwined with Rome itself.

It is true, as we have seen, that the Romans felt that running a province after serving a year in public office in Rome entitled the governor to put something into his pockets. Verres had gone too far, but the basic idea was not considered wrong or unethical, as we would find it. Roman imperium included the right to obtain payment from provinces that Rome had conquered and subdued. There may have been unwritten limits, but not knowing whether Catiline broke them—because we do not know the details of the bribery and corruption charges against him—makes it difficult to evaluate this lawsuit. Nor is it easy to compare it to Verres's case, which had involved larceny on a massive scale. What we know about the conditions of Africa make it extremely unlikely that Catiline could have robbed and defrauded the locals in a manner even remotely similar to what Verres did. The money just was not there, as it had been in the rich island of Sicily. If he had governed the rich coastal cities of Libya, it would be different.

A third issue with the story about the threatened lawsuit is this: the Africans wrote to Rome a letter signaling their intention to file a lawsuit against Catiline, but they did not file a suit. The inaction is puzzling; what explains it? Let us accept that they needed time to gather evidence. But on the strength of that letter, vague though it was, a young, populist senator named Publius Clodius Pulcher brought a lawsuit against Catiline. Clodius was a well known troublemaker, a politician who sought to hog the limelight with grandiose gestures, though he was also an innovative legislator. In this case he appears to have smelled an easy way to make himself better known by marching to the defense of the Africans and going after Catiline, possibly hoping it would be a new Verres case and he, Clodius, would reap renown and glory.* Once Clodius brought the suit, Catiline became politically paralyzed because the law prohibited standing for election while under criminal trial.

Catiline's trial started in November 65 BC, that is, over a year after he had returned. That seems a very long time, but let us allow for delays in Roman bureaucratic paper pushing. The fact is that after that initial declaration of intent to sue, no more seems to have been heard from the Africans. No evidence arrived in Rome. No further letters were received. No solicitor was retained (Clodius had acted on his own initiative; we have no evidence he had been asked to intervene by the Africans). Why not?

The answer might be found among the papers of the man who would become Catiline's enemy within a little over a year: Cicero. In early 64 BC, Cicero wrote to his friend and editor, Titus Pomponius Atticus, that he was thinking of taking on Catiline's defense in the African trial: "I am thinking I might defend in court Catiline, who is going to run for the office of Consul against me. . . . The judges are favourable. If he is let off, I expect he will support me in the election. If he doesn't, that's too bad."

*The information about Clodius relies on W. Jeffrey Tatum, *The Patrician Tribune: Publius Clodius Pulcher* (Chapel Hill: University of North Carolina Press, 1999).

So Cicero, the man who had prosecuted Verres, after hearing the specific charges against Catiline, was willing to dirty his hands and defend the former governor? Since Cicero really wanted to be consul—it would confirm his place in Roman society—and since he was all too aware of the political backlash that might result from his taking on Catiline's brief, there is only one credible explanation for these sentences. In spite of the atrocious charges he would throw at Catiline within a year, at that moment, Cicero thought the case against Catiline was weak enough that he (Cicero) would gain a great deal of publicity with little cost. This was not another Verres, whose depredations Cicero could easily exploit in court and therefore turn the accused into an indefensible crook. This was a man Cicero could deal with, defend, and ensure he was let off. The judges may have been favorable—that suggests Crassus had a hand in it—but no really serious charges corroborated by strong evidence could have been swept under the rug. If there had been a remote chance of that, Cicero's reputation as the lawyer who took the moral high ground, the defender of falsely accused honest men (Sextus Roscius), the unbending prosecutor of corrupt governors, would have been mercilessly replaced by his notoriety as Cicero, the provincial lawyer who was on sale to any aristocratic robber. There would be no coming back from that political grave for a man like Cicero, and he knew it. So his willingness to defend Catiline—in practice it came to nothing, Catiline had a perfectly good defense team, which again suggests he had the money (probably Orestilla's) to pay for it—suggests no more than that Cicero was seeking out an easy and politically rewarding legal victory because the charges were so insubstantial. Which, in the end, likely is the reason why the Africans never actually filed charges: the evidence would not stand up in a court of law.

Politically for Catiline, however, the lawsuit of 66–65 BC was a disaster. Roman law declared that you were banned from running for any public office if you were on trial. This blocked him from presenting his candidacy as consul for 66 (to serve in 65 BC). But it was not strictly the lawsuit for alleged corruption in Africa that disqualified him. The Senate had received no formal communication from a solicitor retained by the Africans detailing his actions and the reasons why they constituted corruption while Catiline was governor (Clodius's suit depended on the Africans' letter, which contained hardly any evidence of corruption). Catiline was disqualified because he had allegedly filed his candidacy late. As far as we know, disqualification on these grounds was rare. Was there a darker motive behind this decision?

We do not know enough about Roman legal procedure to tell whether this disqualification was legally valid. But in general, as a Roman citizen, Catiline had the right to appeal (*provocatio*) against any action to his detriment by public officials. If he did have the right to appeal in this case as well, did he choose to exercise it, and what was the result? We do not know. But we do know that Catiline was not allowed to run for the office of consul in 66 BC.

The man who disqualified Catiline was named Lucius Volcatio Tullius. He was an aristocrat close to the senatorial elite. In that year he was consul and therefore in charge of elections. His decision seems arbitrary and possibly motivated by some other factor. But let us first consider another fact that sheds a rather sinister light on the entire event.

When Catiline was disqualified, the Senate had received no formal filing of a lawsuit. There was a letter of complaint—a pretty standard set of accusations by the people of a province against a governor—but no legal action had yet been undertaken except for Clodius's charge against Catiline based on the Africans' letter of intent to file a lawsuit. If Clodius took this step to gain attention, as we argued, then it is worth remembering that he had had, as far as we know, nothing to do with Africa, and no evidence suggests he had even been there, certainly not during Catiline's governorship.

The act seems gratuitous unless it was meant for some other purpose. And that purpose is obvious: the law prevented anyone undergoing a criminal trial—as a trial for corruption was—from running for any office. If you wanted to make sure that Catiline would be unable to put forth his candidacy not only in 66 BC (for the 65 BC election) but also in 65 BC (for the 64 BC election), this kind of legal initiative would serve your purpose admirably. The lawsuit, however ridiculous or unjustified, was enough, and was used frequently in Rome's political brawls.

Having filed the lawsuit, Clodius did not go after Catiline with the kind of energy we might expect from a prosecuting lawyer, certainly not with the energy that Cicero had displayed in the case of Verres. That is in itself interesting because it suggests Clodius did not really care whether Catiline was acquitted: he only wanted to keep him out of the way for the elections of 65 BC.

And the proof of this is that at some point in the trial, Clodius withdrew his lawsuit against Catiline. That meant in practice that Clodius no longer believed the evidence of Catiline's wrongdoing, assuming he had at some point in the past believed it. The only one who was apparently seriously annoyed with this was Quintus Caecilius Metellus Pius, general and hero of the war against Sertorius in Spain, a relative of Clodius's, and a former supporter of Sulla's. Clodius's withdrawal of the lawsuit made Clodius, his gens, and his party a laughingstock—and Clodius's mother was from the gens Metella, like Quintus himself. So who had talked Clodius into filing a lawsuit?

We cannot be sure, of course, but Clodius was an aristocrat and so was Volcatio Tullius. That in itself means nothing, but it does point the finger of suspicion to the senatorial class, the large landowners who had been defended by Sulla's political program. Was there, for them, a good reason to prevent Catiline from becoming consul? On the surface, it seems unlikely: Catiline had been an officer of Sulla's and had carried out a number of assassinations of populares under cover of the proscription lists. He was an aristocrat whose uncle had plotted with Sulla the overthrow of Marius's dictatorship. He was a senator, and nothing he had done in the Senate had been designed to diminish the power of the senatorial class.

It may seem strange, then, that Volcatio Tullius, consul and president of the Centuriata, the more aristocratic of Rome's assemblies, should rule against the aristocrat Catiline. But Catiline was still seen as Crassus's man, and Crassus had started to move closer to the populares. Never mind that Catiline had commanded Sulla's death squads; that was then, his potential candidacy was now. He was a powerful speaker, not as refined as Cicero but gifted with great, direct, and expressive force, as even his enemy, the historian Sallust, had to concede. Catiline had had a distinguished military career and had risked his life many times for Rome fighting among his enlisted men, and this was an important element in Roman elections. The Romans set great store by how one faced death and ultimately died. A true Roman confronted death with, as Cicero says, a spirit of "haughty defiance," and this Catiline had shown time and again.

We can only conclude that there was something about Catiline that frightened the senatorial class. This kind of effort to delay his candidacy was exceptional, and it cannot be explained by simply saying that he was disliked by the optimates because he was one of the populares. In fact, in the elections of 66 BC, two populares ran for consul: Publius Cornelius Sulla (a distant relation of the dead dictator) and Publius Autronius Paetus. As far as we are aware, no efforts were made to prevent them from running—though things got stickier after their election.

But there was something about Catiline that was just too uncomfortable for the men who sat in the Senate, and possibly for many equites as well. In part it may have been his reputation as a tough guy, someone who went all the way with determination and sangfroid. One historian has described him as someone who "said what he thought and did what he said." In the incestuous world of Roman politics, this was an uncomfortable, even dangerous, new element. After all, this was a political class in which the richest men in the city—who had amassed great wealth by driving untold citizens into debt and grinding poverty—could lead the "popular" party; in which marriage and bloodlines crossed and recrossed political divides, and supposedly opposite factions were regularly in cahoots; and in which the "leftist" party had shown itself to be no more than a bunch of immensely rich landowners without ideological compasses who, through bribery and flattery, got the poor to vote for them. On the Right, equally rich aristocrats saw the republic as their own plaything, denied against all evidence that the poor of their expanding empire had any legitimate complaints to make, and systematically defined all dissent as the act of traitors to the republic. Both sides built up political support by having individual plutocrats throw massive, publicly funded parties for religious festivals or organizing games where slaves fought each other to the death.

In a closed, self-referential environment like this, a man like Catiline could only introduce an element of worrisome disturbance, and that might have been enough to induce Clodius and Volcatio Tullius to try to block his candidacy for 66 and 65 BC. In the elections of 66 BC, when Catiline could not run, the populares candidates Cornelius Sulla and Autronius Paetus faced two optimates, Lucius Manlius Torquatus and Lucius Aurelius Cotta. None of them was an exciting personality: they seem to have been time servers who just needed the consulate as a ticket to then go and rob some province or other.

To Cotta's credit, as praetor in 70 BC, he had introduced the bill to include equites in juries, undoing one of

Sulla's reforms. And one of these juries in 65 BC acquitted Catiline of corruption and depredation of the African colony. No evidence had been found that he had practiced concussio, and if the jury could not be swayed, there really must have been nothing there. But the damage had been done. Catiline had been kept from running for consul for two years. That was probably the objective, since in 66 BC the four contenders were reasonably indistinguishable from one another. None of them had a political program, in the sense of proposing changes in the administration of power or the organization of society. If Catiline had been allowed to run, it seems likely he would have made mincemeat out of all of them. He appears, in that year he returned from Africa, to have had in mind a series of initiatives, mostly still at the level of inchoate ideas rather than a precise political program. But if he had been a candidate, the program might have jelled. All of these ideas were unmistakably dangerous.

Where these ideas came from we do not know. We are not aware of a moment of conversion, like St. Paul is alleged to have had on the road to Damascus. At no point is there evidence that Catiline explicitly renounced his past as Sulla's henchman in favor of becoming an advocate of the poor. It may be that his experience in Africa had an effect on him, throwing in his face the evidence of appalling poverty and suffering. It may be that Aurelia Orestilla, his new wife who came from a rich but not noble family, shared with him what she must have known about the masses of the poor who lived—culturally invisible—in the interstices of newly imperial Rome. It may have been a sense of disgust by the last of the Sergii at the sight of men of his own class prostituting themselves for the privileges conferred by money and power. It may have been all of these in varying mixes.

We do not know. But we do know that after his return from Africa, Catiline had some strange thoughts, and while he could not present them yet as a coherent political program because he had been disqualified from running, he must have talked about them. In reality, his thoughts in 66 BC were harking back sixty or so years, to the reforms initiated by Tiberius and Gaius Gracchus: land redistribution, cancellation or at least significant reduction of debt and interest charges, opening a variety of public offices to the poor. One can imagine the suppressed gasps as senators, wine goblets in their hands, heard this kind of talk. This was more than dangerous talk, it was war talk, civil war, and coming from one of their own, an aristocrat and a senator. Oh, and just as a reminder, the civil war had only just finished fifteen years earlier.

When he was acquitted of concussio in his governorship, Catiline had plenty of time to file his candidacy in early summer 64 BC for the office of consul in 63. There followed six dramatic months that we need to dissect in detail because they show Catiline and his opponents in their true colors.

7

THE ELECTION
OF 66 BC

To UNDERSTAND THE EVENTS OF 64 BC, WE HAVE TO step back a moment to consider the election of 66 BC, in which the consuls and other officials who would be in office the following year, 65 BC, were chosen. The populares candidates, Cornelius Sulla and Autronius Paetus, had won the consular elections. The young Caesar had been elected aedilis, and Crassus had become censor. The populares had scored big, in fact bigger than the electoral results suggest. At the time of the election, Pompey was away from Rome, fighting the never-ending war with Mithridates. This left Crassus and the populares in virtual control of the city. Crassus's prestige was riding high at that moment, not only for the electoral victory but also because only five years earlier he had put an end to Spartacus and his slave revolt with an army financed entirely by himself. If Crassus decided to move, there was nothing standing between him and absolute power.

Something had to be done. At the end of the summer, just after the elections, Manlius Torquatus and Aurelius Cotta, the defeated candidates (optimates both), filed a lawsuit on the grounds that Cornelius Sulla and Autronius Paetus had cheated in the election, buying votes and corrupting the voters. To compensate them for the loss they had suffered, Torquatus and Cotta asked that the results be annulled and they be made consuls.

As an accusation, this charge of buying off the voters was undoubtedly credible: pretty well all candidates bribed voters with food, wine, and cash to ensure their loyalty in the voting Comitia. It is not impossible that Torquatus and Cotta had lost the election only because their bribery had been less abundant or less enticing than what the populares had offered. But they took the initiative to file the suit, knowing that the jury—aristocrats and equites—would take their side. And in fact, Cornelius Sulla and Autronius Paetus were disqualified, and the Senate appointed Torquatus and Cotta as the new consuls: the populares won the election and lost the important offices. If, as seems likely, Crassus had managed to influence the appointment of the judges in Catiline's trial, this time the aristocracy had bested him.

But a man in his position could not accept the outcome of this political maneuvering. So on December 5, 66 BC, he met with his closest associates and prepared a plot to do away with Torquatus and Cotta. The plan they cobbled together seems, from the information we have, almost pathetically juvenile, not to say incompetent. We know who attended the meeting in Crassus's house the night of December 5. First, Catiline and Caesar were there. Then, of course, were Cornelius Sulla and Paetus, the victorious candidates removed by the Senate. With them was Cneus Calpurnius Piso, whose cousin, Calpurnia, was to be Caesar's third wife; Gaius Antonius Hybrida, who was to be the uncle of the Mark Antony who would speak at Caesar's funeral and would later order the murder of Cicero, and Publius Cornelius Lentulus, the stepfather of the same Mark Antony (Hybrida and Lentulus had been expelled from the Senate in 70 BC for "immorality"—i.e., corruption—upon Pompey's request, but as they were both populares that is not surprising); and Publius Sittius Nucerinus, the son of a landed equites family near Naples, not particularly rich but ambitious. There does not appear to have been anybody else. Eight men were going to subvert the political order of Rome and of an empire that stretched from the Black Sea to the Atlantic Ocean and from North Africa to the English Channel. Even with the best will in the world, it was political lunacy, and we know for certain that at least one of the conspirators understood this.

This was the plan that took shape that night: on the day when Torquatus and Cotta were to officially assume their duties as new consuls, that is, on January 1, 65 BC, a group of men led by Catiline would break out of the crowd assembled for the ceremony and kill the usurpers in full public view. Along with the two "fake" consuls, some of the more conservative senators were also to meet their gruesome ends. The "true" consuls, Cornelius Sulla and Paetus, would then intervene, claim their right-

ful position as consuls, and immediately resign in favor
of Crassus, who would accept their entreaties and
become dictator for six months, as the constitution
allowed. Notice the six months: aside from being the traditional duration of office for a dictatorship in times of
emergency, it would bring Crassus's term to an end in
late June, leaving the summer open for new candidates to
file their papers for the next elections. This was meant to
reassure the electorate that Crassus would not be a new
bloodthirsty Sulla. Quite the contrary: he was just
responding to a crisis, preventing a new civil war, and
waiting for people's emotions to calm down after the
Senate's egregious violation of the electoral results.

For his part, Crassus would endorse and assist
Catiline's candidacy for the consulate in the following
year, 64 BC. Caesar would be asked to organize an expedition to annex Egypt, Piso would be given an extraordinary command in Spain where Sertorius's rebellion still
smouldered, and Sittius would be sent to Africa.

The plan was, to put it mildly, silly. The conspirators
did not have the troops to occupy the command centers
of the capital, to control the crowds, or to face down any
army likely to move against them from the nearby territories. They may have had popular support in the city
itself, but unarmed and untrained civilians counted for
close to nothing. Senators were well guarded by highly
trained and experienced soldiers. Even if the conspirators' daggers had found their targets, the chances were
very high that the next deaths would be the conspirators'
themselves. It also seems silly that Crassus would expose
himself to such a farce: if the "true" consuls had, after
the butchery, called on him to become dictator and save

the republic, everybody would have known for certain where this coup d'état was coming from. That awareness had far-reaching political implications, for him and for others. To name just one, Pompey would not be in the east forever, and his revenge was likely to be merciless and swift, as Sulla's had been twenty years earlier. In fact, Crassus risked helping Pompey's rise.

The man who clearly saw the bankruptcy of this scheme was Caesar, who had a very clear tactical mind and a precise sense of where he wanted to go. First of all, his election had not been challenged, so there was no reason for him to take risks. And risks there were plenty: staking life and credibility on this half-baked plot of Crassus's did not appeal to him, but he owed too much money to simply walk out. So he accepted the idea of the plot and agreed to play a primary role in it. But as he did so often in his political career, he kept his own counsel.

It is a bit more difficult to understand Catiline's motivations. He had taken on the role of leader of the murderers, which in itself says a lot about how he was perceived, even among his associates. His reward—Crassus's support for his election to consul for the following year—seems puny in comparison. If he failed, he would be slaughtered before the eyes of the assembled crowds—and that was the nice option: he might have been strangled in the Mamertine Prison* for his efforts,

---

*The Mamertine Prison was a structure dug under the Roman Capitol where alleged criminals were incarcerated waiting for trial or execution. It was not used as a long-term detention center: once a verdict was passed, the accused would be freed, enslaved, or put to death.

not a death you would willingly take on, or, alternatively, nailed to a cross along the Appian Way, an equally unpleasant way to die. What was driving him?

Two elements may explain Catiline's willingness to participate in this harebrained scheme. The first was strictly personal: his involvement with Sulla's death squads suggests an idealistic personality, someone who saw the world in simple, opposite terms. These personalities may become excessively concerned with specific objectives, like the removal of an enemy, without whom something of great value would be restored. And to achieve this objective they may be willing to take risks disproportionate to the rewards that a cold, rational analysis would identify as their ultimate outcome. This may have been an element in Catiline's character, something that made him at the same time generous and intolerant, and would eventually reveal him to be unable to deal with accusations thrown at him by lesser but more cautious and calculating men.

The second possible explanation for Catiline's readiness to play a part in Crassus's insane plan was more political. He had experienced at first hand the injustice of his own exclusion from the consular elections, on what seem nowadays spurious grounds, for two years running. It may not have been the consular office per se he wanted as he took on the role of chief assassin; it was the public demonstration that his own exclusion in the past two years had been nothing other than a grubby, corrupt initiative of the terrified élite that ran Rome. He was an aristocrat and a senator; his family had helped found and manage the city in its early days. If he accepted the kind of impudence displayed by the Senate's disallowing the election victory of Cornelius Sulla and Autronius Paetus, the optimates' faction would from then on have a free hand. That would hollow out the efforts of all the Sergii who had built Rome and written its laws, in effect wiping out his heritage. Besides, a senatorial victory on these terms would silence the voices of protest that he was increasingly hearing, and those were the voices of Roman citizens, men like him, with his pride in being a civis Romanus, one of the conquerors of the world, now beaten into poverty by money-grubbing and dishonest senators. He could not let these voices be silenced for years, maybe forever, as a corrupt and incestuous clique of rich landlords ran the city as they pleased. To this writer, his motivation was admirable, his tactics less so.

Personal and political factors were probably intertwined in Catiline's mind. Killing the "fake" consuls was part of his desire to rebuild an older, stronger Rome, where one political party could not lord it over the population with complete impunity. The political balance had to be maintained, or rather reintroduced, as it had been in the days of the old republic, five centuries earlier, when the Romans had chased out their last king and had established a system of government in which debate and equilibrium defined public action. It was worth risking death for that ideal, or rather for that reality that had once defined Rome. Some things are worth dying for.

For the last of the Sergii, that was probably the final consideration: his own life he could spend with the haughty defiance of a Roman aristocrat, but he carried within himself a responsibility for the lives of others, and that responsibility he could not ignore. Catiline made this explicit in his final letter to Quintus Lutatius Catulus, the only document we have from him (the letter was read aloud in the Senate in 62 BC, and Sallust copied it): "I have taken onto myself," he wrote, "as has been my wont in the past, the defence of the oppressed." To him, the oppressed were the Roman citizens abused by the senatorial elite. Slaves, as we will see, were not among them.

But the plan did not work—mercifully, we might add, for if it had there would probably have been a massacre before the Senate building, likely followed by a new civil war. The agreement was that Catiline would take the men willing to strike at the consuls and senators to the Forum, and there he would wait for Caesar to give them the signal: he was supposed to let his cape slip from his shoulders at the opportune moment. How many men Catiline brought with him, and who they were, is unclear, possibly a few dozen. They may have been common criminals or paid killers, or they may have been political idealists like Catiline. Likely they were a bit of both, and on that chilly January 1, there they were, their daggers concealed under their tunics, watching the thin figure of Caesar across the road as the senators, guards, and consuls walked in solemn procession to the Senate building, wearing their symbols of office. But across the road Caesar held onto his cape, clutching it around his shoulders as a cold wind blew. He never let it slip.

Catiline was paralyzed: without Caesar's signal, he could not start. In the gathered crowds he looked in vain for Crassus to see if he would give him a sign. But Crassus was not there. The conspirators stood without knowing what to do next.

Puzzled, in the end they simply went home.

Crassus called a new meeting and proposed the same plan for February 5. But as so often happens when secret plans are concerned, delay meant relay: the Senate heard that some attempt on the consuls' lives had been planned and gave the consuls an armed escort. And the senators must have heard more, because they appointed Sittius ambassador to the king of Mauretania. Cneus Calpurnius Piso was given the role of general for Spain.

On February 5, things went even worse: Caesar was simply not there, and neither was Crassus. In any event, not all of the conspirators had arrived, which may mean someone had told them off. In the end, Catiline, on his own initiative, gave the signal, but too few men were on his side. They moved against the procession and there was a bit of pushing and shoving with the consuls' body-guards, but by then the plan had been discovered. The group of conspirators simply came apart, and the suspicions that surrounded Crassus seriously damaged his ability to pull strings. Corrupt and unethical though it might have been, Rome had survived an attempted coup d'état without bloodshed. Life could go on.

Why were Catiline and the others not arrested? In the first place, nothing had really happened: shoving and pushing a soldier was not an offense (the bodyguards were military men, not police). Nobody had been killed or even lightly wounded. In addition, arresting a Roman citizen involved having a lawsuit against him, and nobody filed one. The public prosecutor could not arrest a Roman citizen without a lawsuit pending against him. The prosecutor could file a suit himself, but what would the grounds have been? The intentions of the few conspirators there may have been clear to those present, but that is not evidence. In sum, February 5 was almost a nonevent.

This whole conspiracy—called Catiline's first conspiracy, even though nothing suggests he initiated it—appears to be the product of a deluded brain. But that might be taking it far too superficially. It may not be impossible—though there is no evidence for this, so what follows is pure speculation—that some of the conspirators actually wanted the attempt to fail theatrically, ending in bloodshed. They may have wished for the blood to be, first and foremost, Catiline's. He may have been a difficult character to deal with, a man who lacked political finesse and saw the complexity of life in the newly forming empire in starkly simplistic terms. Those were the very qualities you could exploit if you gave him a well-defined objective and described it as the source of all the moral and political decay he was always going on about. Go kill those bastards, they have ruined the city. Yes, sir! In the meanwhile, hold your cape tightly against the chilly winds of idealism.

This is not to blame Caesar. Or Crassus or anybody else. But the plan was stupid, and it failed because someone realized it was. Rome, tense and filled with rumors but as yet unbloodied, marched toward spring 64 BC. Pompey was doing well in the east, Sertorius and Spartacus were dead. The campaign against the pirates had scored some important victories. It was time to look forward to spring 64 BC, rejoice in the blossoms of the almond and cherry trees, and prepare for the long, hot summer. For Catiline, it was time to file his candidacy for the 64 BC election that would determine the consuls of 63 BC.

8

POLITICAL INTRIGUE

SPRING CAME, AND IN EARLY SUMMER, JUST AS THE peasants and slaves of the landholdings in the great alluvial plane of the Tiber were bringing in the grain crop, Catiline was at last able to file his papers for his candidacy to the office of consul. He also convened his election committee, in his house on the Aventine Hill, on June 1, 64 BC. We have a partial list of those who were there: Publius Lentulus, Publius Autronius, Lucius Cassius Longinus, Gaius Cethegus, Publius and Servius Sulla (the dictator's nephews), Lucius Vergunteius, Quintus Ennius Chilo, Marcus Porcius Laecae, Lucius Calpurnius Bestia, and Quintus Curius. These were all senators, and, except for Curius, young men. There were some equites, such as Marcus Fulvius Nobilior, Lucius Statilius, Publius Gabinius Capito, and Gaius Cornelius. With them were many even younger people of varying social status, and a number of farmers' representatives from different towns and provinces in Italia.

As the long evening of early summer drew to a close, Catiline spoke to his election committee, promising debt relief and land reform if elected consul. He talked of the sorrow he had seen on the land that, if handed over to those who farmed it, would have produced more than enough to feed Rome and Italia, instead of enriching a few greedy landlords, allowing them to flatten mountains and drain lakes for their own pleasure of building luxurious villas. He declared himself the champion of the oppressed (*miserorum causa*), a phrase he was to use again and again in the electoral campaign over the coming months. He set out in effect a very radical plan of economic and social reform, and it may seem strange to those who have a sense of the geography of Rome that he chose to do it from the Aventine. The Aventine Hill was then—as it is now—one of the prime bits of real estate in Rome. Situated along the Tiber but far to the west of the city center, it rose above the fumes and smells of the increasingly crowded city. It overlooked the course of the river as it flowed toward the sea and was always blessed by fresh winds that kept the air clear and pleasant. Today it is the location of many embassies.

Radical proposals from the Aventine? But Catiline was never an opponent of wealth: he objected to property amassed by theft and abuse. He did not have to play the role of the poor radical politician: he could be an aristocrat who saw the abuses and wished to remedy them. Actually, that was exactly his task: as an aristocrat, he owed the poor protection and, if necessary, as it was in his time, redress.

At the meeting of June 1, and later during the election campaign, Catiline delivered speech after speech with a consistent message: only I can understand you. Only I share your poverty and your worries. Do not put your trust in the rich, who only use you for their own power and privileges. Apparently one sentence that Catiline repeated over and over made a huge impression: "In the Roman Republic, there are two bodies. One is frail and sickly with an empty head; the other is strong and healthy, but has no head. I intend to be that head, if I can show I deserve to be, as long as I live." This was a bomb: he was saying, in fact, I will take over the leadership of the strong but aimless body and lead it. The strong and aimless body was the urban poor. He did not say against whom he would lead it: that was clear. This was fighting talk more dangerous than Gaius and Tiberius Gracchus had ever used.

Knowledge of the meeting and the speech spread quickly. The senatorial aristocracy cast about for a solution, a way to stop this traitor to his class, this madman who wanted to revolutionize the republic. They felt themselves in a danger more serious and worrisome than any they had faced before. There had been nothing quite so reckless in the history of the republic.

We do not know who hit on the idea, but the senators asked Cicero, whom they despised, to run. They assured him of full financial and political support in defeating this madman.

Cicero spoke eloquently against Catiline in the consular campaign of 64 BC. He dug up the Gratidianus affair, the conspiracy of 66–65, and even mentioned his own sister-in-law, the vestal Fabia, and the sexual contacts Catiline had supposedly had with her. Never mind that Catiline had been tried and acquitted: what mattered was to paint him as a depraved, immoral beast, someone from whom you could expect nothing but blood and mayhem.* However, Cicero conveniently forgot to mention that a few months earlier, in early 64 BC, in fact, he was "thinking I might defend in court Catiline, who is going to run for the office of Consul." Evidently Catiline stopped being a potential political ally and became a depraved monster sometime between winter and summer 64 BC.

It was at that point that Cicero struck a deal with Hybrida.

Beside Catiline, six other candidates ran in 64 BC for the two positions of consul: Marcus Tullius Cicero, Publius Sulpicio Galba, and Gaius Licinius Sacerdos ran for the optimates, and Gaius Antonius Hybrida, Lucius Cassius Longinus, and Quintus Cornificius for the populares. When Catiline filed his papers to run, Longinus withdrew his candidacy so as not to take votes away from the other populares. Galba, Sacerdos, and Cornificius were reckoned to be weak candidates, lacking a clear support base and name recognition. The real race was likely to be between Cicero, Hybrida, and Catiline. Cicero was supported by most of the senatorial élite and the equites. Crassus, Caesar, and the populares plumped for Hybrida and Catiline. But there was a stumbling block, of which Catiline seems to have been unaware: Hybrida could be easily blackmailed because of his ejection from the Senate some six years earlier.

---

*Walter Allen provides a very convincing analysis of Cicero's motivations. "In Defence of Catiline," *Classical Journal* 34, 1938.

What had happened was that Hybrida had been one of Sulla's cavalry commanders during the war against Mithridates, and he had remained in Greece to keep peace and order after Sulla's departure for Rome. In reality, Hybrida had then happily devoted himself to plundering the Greek countryside and committing atrocities on the local population, including maiming and torture, that earned him the nickname Hybrida ("half-beast"). Pompey in this case had been quite right when he asked for, and obtained, Hybrida's removal from the senatorial rank in 70 BC. But it was for naught, because the following year, Hybrida was elected tribune, which meant he again joined the Senate.

Hybrida could be blackmailed easily because anyone knowing about his Greek escapades could file a lawsuit against him. As we have seen in Catiline's case, that would have stopped him in his tracks, possibly for years, because the evidence was that (unlike Catiline in Africa) he really had behaved brutally in Greece. Under these circumstances, it was not difficult for a man gifted with a silver tongue and the reputation of a tough prosecutor of governors who had mistreated their charges to make him an offer he could not refuse. To keep me quiet, said this man, tell your supporters to vote for me as well as for you. After all, they have to vote for two names, there are two consuls. Let them vote for Hybrida first, but tell them their second choice has to be Marcus Tullius Cicero. Through his mouth, the senatorial élite was expressing its own preference for a man who could be controlled, even if he came from the ranks of the populares, over a genuine threat, an independent fighter who seemed ready to throw all their privileges to the wind.

Hybrida went along with Cicero's proposal, and his acceptance of this blackmail provides us with irrefutable evidence of the incestuous nature of Roman political power. Cicero the conservative could strike a deal with Hybrida the revolutionary and would-be assassin of a few months earlier in order to keep things just as they were. In the meanwhile, he could denounce Catiline, another member of the assassin group, as an evil maniac. Politics is the art of the possible, but in this case it seems to have been the art of the unlikely.

When the ballots were counted in late summer, Cicero came first, followed by Hybrida, who beat Catiline by a handful of votes. He had missed the consular office again.

This unexpected defeat must have stunned Catiline. He had probably never imagined that there could be an agreement between a conservative and a candidate of the populares; Catiline just did not appear to have been that kind of man. To him, wrong was wrong, end of story. The idea that Hybrida might have been on sale probably never crossed his mind. We might cynically suggest that someone with this kind of personality should not have gone into politics, but that is our own bias, twenty centuries later. He had been steeped from birth into a different bias—you did what you said—and there was no room for personal prostitution in that. Or, just possibly, he may have taken the result as an actual vote of confidence, a vote he had lost. He had to try again. As soon as possible, he decided to file papers for his candidacy in the consular elections of 63 BC.

Before he could do so, Caesar hit out. As a former supporter of Marius's—remember, he had had to get out of the city quickly when Sulla had taken over for the last time—he got the Senate to put on trial some of those who had committed murder under Sulla's command. Among them was Catiline, for the old story of Gratidianus's death. But the court could find no proof, and Catiline was absolved. Given how the Senate was feeling about Catiline at that point, if there had been a shred of proof to link him to Gratidianus's death, it is impossible to believe the jurors—all of them senators because Catiline was a senator—would have absolved him. Nice though it is to be declared not guilty, Catiline now knew he was on his own: Caesar had come out in the open, and the populares were against Catiline. His only supporters were a few radical youths and the farmers who saw in him the resolution to the old land problem they had struggled with in vain for so long.

But the question is, why did Caesar strike right then? In part it may have been because he realized that Catiline was not just another aristocrat who wanted to pin on his toga the label of the populares. Catiline was his own man, a real radical and revolutionary, and from Caesar's and Crassus's point of view, ultimately not manageable. This seemed to be a man who was not afraid to stir up some old wounds and exhume deep collective resentments on his way to power. And what he would do with that power did not really bear thinking about. Not if you were an aristocrat, that is.

If Caesar wanted the mantle of the next leader of the populares once Crassus died (he would turn fifty-three that year, a relatively young age for us but not so for the Romans), he had better try to embroil Catiline in something that would slow him down and possibly paralyze him for good. Besides, Caesar was heavily in debt to

Crassus, and his political career depended on the older man's willingness to extend more credit. Land reform would have cut Crassus's income and with it his ability to finance Caesar.

By then Catiline's motivation may have begun to change. Yes, the fortune of the gens Sergia still weighed on him, but with that a new concern had taken shape. The irrefutable poverty and misery of the oppressed he would champion (*"publicam miserorum causam pro mea consuetudine suscepi"*)—something he stressed in his letter to his friend before going into his final battle— had probably drawn a parallel with his family's conditions. The solution to this unspeakable set of circumstances in which contemporary Rome had been sunk by greed and corruption was not to plot for the establishment of an autocrat, as his uncle Bellienus had evidently believed in supporting Sulla.* The solution was to throw the whole political structure overboard and start again. Catiline, wrote Dio Cassius many years later, "wanted to change the Roman constitution."

It is one thing to want to change the constitution; it is quite another to bring forth the legal initiatives necessary to raise the question in the open. Some action must be taken to force the established order to explain why

---

*Bellienus was involved in the lawsuit brought by Julius Caesar against Sulla's associates at the time of the proscription lists (82–81 BC). The trial, in which Bellienus and others were involved and eventually condemned, appears to have been an attempt to intimidate Catiline in preparation for an eventual showdown with Caesar over the leadership of the populares. Catiline was not involved in the trial, except marginally over the Gratidianus allegations, but Caesar's warning shot is clear. See Fini, 77–79.

things should stay as they are. For the powerful, this is a trap: whatever their defense of the status quo, they have to come to terms with a deeper danger. In practice, they have to articulate an explanation of conservative politics that will appeal to the population at large: in attempting this, they face the danger that their explanation may be unconvincing or transparently self-serving. Depending on your political goals, that may be disastrous or out-standing. But as a revolutionary, you have to force them out into the open. Provoke them, attack them, goad them into a heavy-handed reaction. If you do this again and again, you can ratchet up your attacks, knowing the established order will have to match you and, if it ever hopes to defeat you, bring the entire weight of police power to bear. If your propaganda has been skilful enough, their reaction will be your victory. But all this depends on that first step: asking why we should keep things as they are. Do poverty, destitution, desperation count for nothing, Senator? The élite can deny the existence of abysmal living conditions, or they can accept them and say pious things about helping the poor. Either way, you have them.

It's that first kick that must be well aimed.

One possible strategy is to introduce a legislative measure that is popular yet so outrageous that the men in charge of the government will be forced to reject it with a clear set of arguments, which the attackers can then sink one by one. It's an old strategy, one that is intu-itively understood by demonstrators everywhere. A slo-gan painted on city walls during the Tunisian revolution of 2011 said, *"Soyez raisonnables: demandez l'impossi-ble"*—Be realistic: demand the impossible.

The drawback, of course, is that the established order can, if it is clever enough, then paint you as a madman. It takes a good propagandist to pull that off. Rome's optimates had one: Cicero.

9

ENTER CATO

THE BILL TO PROVOKE THAT KIND OF DEFENSE WAS reasonably easy to write: land redistribution was a ready-made issue lying there for the plucking. The provocation could be summed up in two words: *tabulae novae* ("new tables"). It meant rewriting the records listing all property ownership and all debts tied to real estate and individuals. These were the economic basis of Roman society, and changing them was sure to elicit a strong reaction from senators and equites.

The only problem was that Catiline could not introduce bills, that being a power of the tribunes. But on December 10, 64 BC, less than a month before Cicero and Hybrida were to be installed as consuls for the year 63, Publius Servilius Rullus, tribune of the people, introduced the Lex Servilia, a profoundly radical land-reform bill whereby the Roman state would sell its land possessions outside Italia and use the money to buy properties in Italia itself and redistribute them to the landless poor. Although the law did not give the government power to force the sale of Italic land, in effect the government could bring very strong pressure to bear on private landowners to force them to sell specific tracts of land. Compensation would be managed by a commission of ten men (Decemviri) who would also control the distribution of the land to the poor and the settlement of the beneficiaries. These were immense powers that would hollow out the Roman governing system—Tabulae Novae with a vengeance, though not as radical as the Gracchus brothers' land-reform bills of sixty years earlier. In a way, the most dangerous part of the Lex Servilia was that in order to sell publicly owned lands, it had to be determined what lands were public, and that would expose powerful men as having seized public land for their own use (and paying no taxes on it because they did not own it).

The bill was clever: not all Italic land was to be redistributed. The areas subject to the forced sales were listed, and not surprisingly they included parts of Italia where the richest landowners had massive properties—that was the deliberate provocation. Rullus and whoever was behind him—probably Catiline, as we shall see in a moment—wanted to have the richest men in the Republic explain why they lived in unimaginable luxury while the people whose land they had acquired by doubtful means suffered in the filth of the poor quarters of Rome. This was perfect as a revolutionary ploy: very few of the superrich could describe how they had seized thousands of acres of land. Their words would be their own condemnation.

Some exceptions were planned for in the Lex Servilia, one of them being the lands of Etruria (modern-day Tuscany), where Sulla's veterans had been settled. Another exception was the land farmed on behalf of the Roman government by King Jempsale of Mauretania. He had been Catiline's friend ever since the latter's governorship in Africa.

As a side issue, nobody appears to have considered what the effects would be of putting so much land on sale all at the same time: the collapse of land prices would damage the remaining smallholders above all else, and their inability to repay their loans would have pervasive consequences on financial institutions, on credit to tradesmen and craftsmen, on transport, communication, and employment, in effect bringing down the whole economy of Rome. But this apparent lack of forethought may actually have been a sign that the bill was meant to stir up trouble, not to be implemented. Someone needed to provoke the Senate and equestrian élites.

Who was that? Who had designed a bill that would necessarily bring about a hard reaction by the moneyed classes? Not Julius Caesar, who could be a demagogue when he needed to but would never have attacked the hand that fed his ambitions, that is, Crassus. Also, as an ally of Marius's who had avoided Sulla's proscription lists, Caesar would not have defended those who had benefited from Sulla's land policy, that is, Sulla's veterans settled in Etruria. No leader of the populares was likely to have helped Rullus in preparing the bill, pretty well for the same reasons. Certainly no member of the senatorial clique would have had anything to do with it. Rullus may have done most of the drafting, but that detail about exempting Jempsale seems very telling.

The bill aroused the fury of virtually all senators. Cicero gave four long speeches against it (one might have been enough, but the opportunity was too good to pass up), and the other tribune of the people serving with Rullus was paid off by the aristocracy to threaten a veto. The bill never came to a vote. But the word spread that someone in Rome was trying to redistribute land. To the farmers who had just won their citizenship—and with it the right to vote—and who were hungry for land, this man was a hero. The heavy debt that made their lives miserable meant it would only make sense for them to come down to Rome and vote if this man—whoever he was—ever ran again. This man was, almost certainly, Catiline.

Catiline certainly talked about debts and land reform during the election campaign of 63 BC for the office of consul in 62. This was serious business, and he lost the support of the men he most needed: Crassus and Caesar. We know he lost their support because in those elections, the two of them openly supported two other populares candidates: Decimus Junius Silanus and Lucius Licinius Murena, another veteran of Sulla's war against Mithridates. Beside these two, the candidates were Servius Sulpicius Rufus, who had studied with Cicero, and Catiline. Cicero managed the election as consul in office.

After the candidacy papers were filed in early summer 63 BC, Crassus and Caesar gave Catiline the cold shoulder, but Cicero went well beyond that.

In the hot summer of 63 BC, Rome was overrun by farmers who had come to support their man, Catiline. They chanted and demonstrated up and down the streets, as their fathers had done thirty years earlier to win the right to Roman citizenship. Those demonstrations had been the harbingers of a civil war, and to the senatorial mind there was nothing to distinguish these uncouth masses speaking an imperfect Latin from the unwashed mob that had disturbed the republic three decades earlier. Together with these interlopers came the poor of Rome itself, crushed by their own debts. Thirty years earlier the poor had fought the demonstrators over the citizenship issue. This time they took their side—and they were all for Catiline.

But the farmers were in the main poor people for whom traveling to Rome was expensive. They could only remain there for a brief period of time. They had to return to their lands and bring in the grape harvest and, a few weeks later, the olive harvest. These were their main cash crops, so for them the alternative was that over the coming winter their families would run out of cash and starve. Without the farmers, the poor of Rome would relapse into their accustomed apathy. Besides, some of them had been grumbling that a land reform would force them to move away from the city and go work in the fields, foregoing the distributions of food and wine and the free games.

However many of the Roman poor took this attitude, the farmers were vocal, possibly threatening, and unwilling to be restrained. With the city overrun by unruly, foul-mouthed masses, Cicero claimed Rome's public order was being threatened. By his authority as consul, he delayed the election by a number of weeks, ostensibly until things calmed down.

But even as consul, Cicero could not delay the elections without approval from the Senate, so he called a meeting to define when the voting was to take place.

Catiline, as a senator, was present, and Cicero asked him to explain the speeches he had made during the campaign. Those were, he implied, the source of the unrest that Rome now faced, with potentially serious consequences. Catiline sneered.

He stood up and said again what he had already said in his private meetings. He spoke of the "two bodies. One is frail and sickly with an empty head; the other is strong and healthy, but has no head." He knew which he would lead.

Spoken in front of the senators, this line caused a stir: the accusation was too obvious to ignore. Catiline, having in effect told them they were a bunch of corrupt exploiters, walked out of the Senate chamber amid complete, stunned silence.

The only one who was willing to react to this attack by Catiline was Marcus Porcius Cato, a conservative senator who a few days later faced Catiline in the street and berated him. How dare he encourage rebellion and hatred between the classes? Catiline, apparently, looked at Cato without batting an eye. "If any of you," he growled, "try to set a fire against me, I won't fight it with water, but with destruction." He was boasting because he did not have the manpower, but no doubt his intention was real.

As Cicero had planned, the delay in the voting approved by the Senate was fatal for Catiline: one by one, the farmers from the Greek cities of the south and the Etruscans, the Umbri, the Samnites, the Volscii, and the Ligures packed up and went home. They could stay no longer: grapevines and olive trees were calling them back. They left without voting, before the summer ended. The road was long, and thanks to Cicero's dishonesty, their time had run out. In late summer, Silanus and Murena were elected consuls. Catiline came in third. Caesar was elected praetor.

But a few days after the results were announced, Sulpicius, the other defeated consular candidate, accused Murena of buying off the electors by distributing money. His accusation was supported by an unlikely individual, the same conservative senator who had faced Catiline in the street: Marcus Porcius Cato.

Cato was a man out of his time. His great grandfather, whose name he shared, had intellectually led the Roman fight against Carthage. The Older Cato's speeches were obsessively punctuated by his one-liner—"*Ceteroque censeo Carthaginem delendam esse*" ("In any case I think Carthage must be destroyed")—no matter what the topic under discussion may have been. If it hadn't been for Rome's life-and-death struggle with Carthage, it might have become a joke.

With an ancestor like that, and because of the importance of tradition to the Roman gens, the younger Cato did not have an easy personality: he was self-righteous, compulsively law-abiding, quick to pass judgement on others, keenly aware of injustice and abuse of power, and contemptuous of what he saw as irresponsible behavior. The family had been close to Sulla: his uncle had married Sulla's daughter Cornelia. The Catos may have been on what we now call the political Right, but in a more fundamental way they were purists in the sense of feeling a strong connection with what they thought had been old Rome, the simple and democratic (as they perceived it) city their own ancestors had helped shape. In a way they were close to what we know of the Sergii, though much wealthier. Their Rome had been a city of straightforward people bound by strong, firm laws, where wealth and conspicuous consumption were held in disdain. Cato himself went around in a simple tunic, never missed a meeting of the Senate, was always punctual. A great man, probably, but not one it would be easy to like.

Cato lived with almost ostentatious simplicity even though he had inherited pots of money. What mattered to him was the Senate, the laws of his city, and their foundation in philosophy. As senator he joined the conservative aristocratic faction and continuously protested in the chamber that Rome was moving away from the stern purity of its roots. Once, this landed him in the soup with Caesar, whom Cato had seen reading a letter while the Senate was debating important matters. Cato stood up and berated Caesar for not paying attention, going so far as to suggest that this lack of interest may have indicated that Caesar was thinking of betraying Rome. Without a word, Caesar passed the letter to Cato, who took it and read it aloud: it was a love letter from Caesar's mistress, Servilia, a woman of cheerfully easy morals. She was also Cato's half-sister.

That this intolerant, proud aristocrat should have objected to Murena's fraudulent election may seem strange. After all, if Murena was found guilty and removed from his office as consul, Catiline would replace him. But for Cato this was secondary: the important point was that the law be upheld. The fact was that Cato and Catiline had more in common than they realized: they were both aristocrats who objected to the corruption and sleaze into which Rome had fallen. Both were physically brave, capable of great efforts, plainspoken. Both saw the world in simple, contrasting terms. And yet they disliked each other.

For Cato, the Murena issue had brought out two problems of which he was well aware but had probably never had to confront so openly and simultaneously. The first was the petty bribery with which rich (or indebted) aristocrats or equites attracted poor voters: the games, the shows, the free distributions of food and wine in clay vessels that bore the candidate's name.* Cato himself had had to resort to this kind of advertising, as it was the only way to spread his name among the voters and, more importantly, the names of the well-known politicians who supported him—a form of endorsement we still use today. But Murena had not just given away a few beans or glasses of wine, which could be tolerated: he had distributed money. One was a form of throwing a party; the other was bribery. One may have been in bad taste; the other was illegal. There was, to Cato's mind, a big difference between them.

Cato felt that Murena should be disqualified, and if that meant his office of consul would be taken over by Catiline, well, so be it. But the Roman elite did not see it that way. First of all, they could not share Cato's moral outrage: they had all done the same as Murena during their political careers, and who was this young whipper-

---

*Many of these cups still exist: in Rome's Museo Nazionale Romano at the Baths of Diocletian, in beautiful juxtaposition, a cup that encourages voters to elect Cato as a tribune sits side by side with one on which Cassius Longinus expresses his earnest hope that they will vote for his friend Catiline as consul.

snapper (in 63 BC Cato was just over thirty) to start harassing them? Second, Rullus's land-reform bill had put the fear of the gods into them.

The trial instigated by Sulpicius's charge opened in the second half of November 63 BC. The senatorial aristocracy and equites had brought out the biggest guns they could get hold of to defend Murena: Cicero and Crassus. That a conservative lawyer would stand side by side with the leader of the populares in the same intensely political lawsuit casts an interesting light on the nature of Roman politics. Ideological differences were secondary. Politics was a game of personalities where powerful men attracted groups of followers not so much because they were convinced of their leader's wisdom or position, but because they expected significant benefits from his eventual victory. That had been the case between Marius and Sulla: it is difficult to pinpoint exact policy differences between them or their followers. Perhaps Marius's followers were more tied to the memory of Tiberius and Gaius Gracchus, but that was not true of all of Marius's men, and in any event, real differences with Sulla were not wide, the proof being that for all his talk, Marius never attempted a land reform. Crassus, supposedly a leader of the populares, had used his wealth—mostly derived from the indebtedness of those same populares—to smash Spartacus. A few years later, another leader of the populares, Caesar, marched on Rome with his army and seized power, something that Sulla, a conservative aristocrat, had tried to make impossible through a series of reforms that were soon cast aside.

Personality-based politics is inevitably corrupt because it relies on doing personal favors. There is, of course, a personalist element in all politics, but in first century BC Rome there seems to have been little else. That is what Cato was railing against.

Rullus's land-reform bill does not seem to have bothered Cato overmuch, unlike other aristocrats or equites. He may have disapproved of it because it created a commission of land redistribution with dictatorial powers, and that went against the grain of the man. But what really mattered to him overall was the restoration of the old Rome, where ethical considerations ruled above all else and people sacrificed themselves for the good of the republic. A more cynical age might laugh, but these were terribly important elements of Cato's makeup. That was why he fulminated in the Senate against the impropriety of Cicero, consul of the republic, intervening in a criminal case that related to the elections that Cicero himself had been responsible for. As I've said, you may not like Cato, but you have to respect his integrity.

In any event, Cicero remained as defense attorney, the trial—such as it was—went ahead, and Murena was found not guilty. Aside from the scandalous verdict, this meant there was nothing the senatorial élite would not do to keep Catiline out of office.

Then events started taking a turn for the worse.

10

The Catiline
Conspiracy

The trial against Murena had been started by Cato and Sulpicius. After the election results were announced, evidence emerged that the other consul-elect, Silanus, had also paid money (Crassus's, presumably) for votes. No charges were ever laid against Silanus, and in any event they would not have mattered: if the jurors found Murena not guilty, they were likely to find Silanus equally not guilty. The verdict revealed the elections of the republic for what they were: a sham.

At that point, something in Catiline snapped.

He had played the democratic game for years, accepting ludicrous legal challenges and fighting them in good faith. Not one of them had stuck. He had kept presenting himself for one office after the other with a clear record. But after Cicero's agreement with Hybrida and the mockery that Cicero himself had made of the elections for 63 BC, there could be no belief in Rome's electoral system.

Add to this the Murena verdict, and it is easy to understand why someone with a personality like Catiline's would decide to abandon legality. Only violent action, he appears to have decided, could get anywhere. He had built a large base of support among the Italic populations, had some senators on his side, and a large portion of the Roman poor voted for him. Not all, let us be clear: only those who had not yet been thoroughly corrupted by years of free wine and free food handed out by senators and equites in search of electoral success. Those among the poor who voted for him were those who could still remember having the dignity of practicing a trade and being economically independent. These sought a return to their previous lives, before they had been squashed by debts owed to the powerful. Many had been too deeply bought by the free distributions of grain and wine and resented the very idea that they would have to work. But there still were impoverished free men who hoped for a leader who would articulate their demands and lead them to the reclaiming of their lands.*

The only group that was by and large impervious to Catiline's appeal were the equites, whose fortunes depended on loans at interest and who lacked that older

---

*Walter Allen argues that Catiline was planning to use these voters to break the two-party system and introduce a third, seriously reformist party. "In Defence of Catiline." The idea is intriguing, but the evidence is scant.

sense of connection to the poor that many senators descended from ancient families tended to have. Only four equites had participated in the electoral committee meeting of June 1, 64 BC, as opposed to a dozen senators—who overall were considerably fewer in Rome than the equites.

And then there were young people. These came from all social levels: there were the children of senators and of unemployed poor, of skilled tradesmen and small landholders, of moneylenders and rich aristocrats. Catiline's appeal to the youth of republican Rome is easy to understand: the craving for adventure suffused by an idealistic sense of righting wrongs and establishing a society of free and equal citizens, perhaps facing danger and risking their own lives in the process, was without comparison the driving force of these young men for many of whom everything had always been easy. This is an unequalled quest for young people, rich or poor, that over the centuries all kinds of scoundrels and dictators have learned to exploit to their advantage.

The Roman historian Sallust, who was probably Catiline's bitterest enemy and denigrator, even more than Cicero, wrote of these youths that they had all they needed to have a good time and chose to pursue uncertainty over safety and devote themselves to war rather than peace. To his way of thinking, this was a mind-boggling decision, one that could only be understood in terms of perversity and an evil influence—that was, in fact, a depraved subversion of the natural order of things. And the evil influence could only have come from one man: Catiline.

It may be opportune to put Sallust's comment in context: some fifteen years after Catiline's conspiracy,
Sallust endeared himself to Caesar by organizing supply
systems during the war to mop up the remnants of
Pompey's army. In return, Caesar appointed him governor of Libya, which by then had been transformed from
an allied state, as it was in Catiline's time, to a simple
province of the empire. In his office as governor of
Libya, Sallust systematically extorted all he could from
the Libyans and amassed a huge fortune. Only Caesar's
influence prevented him from being tried as Verres had
been. Even so, Sallust was forced to return to Rome. His
political career was over, and he spent his time playing in
his enormous gardens on the Quirinal Hill. From all this
we can gather that this fearless defender of Roman law
and order against Catiline's subversion considered extor-
tion and theft to be the worthy goal of rich young people.

Still another social group joined Catiline, and it may
be surprising, depending on your perspective, given the
conditions of the time: women flocked to the movement.

In Roman society during the first century BC, women
were not exactly held in high esteem. Yes, they were protected, kept separate, revered as the bringers of life. But
they were hidden in the inner parts of the house (at least
among the aristocracy). A few, like the vestals, were
respected in their function as conduits of some divine
will, but overall they were really no more than chattel.

However, it appears that Catiline had defined his
political program not only in terms of debt cancellation
and land reform, but eventually in a broader framework,
aiming at a general social equality that appealed to the

much abused and disregarded women of Rome. Many women became his supporters, helped raise funds, and hide weapons, even though they could neither be elected nor vote. There is some evidence that those who helped the conspiracy were, not surprisingly, the women belonging to the upper classes: cultured, intelligent, capable individuals who probably saw in Catiline's program a means of changing their own position in life. Among them we know one name, Sempronia, a person of considerable accomplishments.

In a time when women were mostly illiterate and confined to the restricted duties of child-care and home making, Sempronia could read and write both Latin and Greek, was skilled in music and dancing. Though these may not seem much to us, knowing about music revealed a cultivated person. These were abilities that few men had, and possibly only a handful of women. They were the marks of an intellectual, someone who could express human emotions by means of sound and movement. Knowledge of Greek exposed her to the vast complexity of thoughts and inquiring philosophy that came from the east, so that Sempronia can be pictured as a new kind of woman in the still tradition-bound Roman society. A new woman about whom there hung a bit of the whiff of scandal because she was so different from the staid, traditional Roman matrons. Her name suggests she came from one of Rome's oldest aristocratic families, the gens Sempronia, who were related by marriage to the gens Cornelia and the gens Licinia, again the gilded top of the aristocracy. She had married Decimus Junius Brutus, a descendant of the revolutionary Brutus who had chased Rome's last king out of the city in the sixth century BC.

Their son, Decimus Junius Brutus Albinus, helped organize the plot that did away with Caesar less than twenty years later. This was not a fashionably radical-chic upper-class family but a rich family with revolutionary ideas that once again were deeply felt, even though it seems that Sempronia's husband was unaware of her involvement with Catiline's lot.

We have no idea how many women like Sempronia there were, how often intelligent, aristocratic women became involved in the conspiracy. But they were there, each one of them, according to Cicero, no better than a prostitute. Poor women were unlikely to do anything of the sort because they were simply too ground down by their daily chores to even be aware of Catiline and his ideas, and in any event, the working classes have always tended to be the most socially conservative elements, if for no other reason than as a form of protection.

There may not have been many Sempronias in Rome itself. Elsewhere, the numbers were probably considerable. In particular, in Etruria, archaeological and artistic evidence shows women of high social status engaged in what appears to be discussion on a par with men. Some Roman writers expressed stunned disbelief at the manners and morals of the Etruscan women, who were known to go out of their house unaccompanied, faced down men's stares "without blushing," took part in banquets lying side by side with male guests on the couches that were used during the serving of meals, talked politics, art, philosophy, and religion, and often had sexual relations with their servants or even slaves.

Now that was depravity beyond all belief. Such women could only encourage immorality, perversion, and social confusion, enticing men to perform acts of such scandalous degeneracy that they could not even be mentioned. As Rosa Luxemburg was well aware, sexual and political rebellion are twin sisters. With these antecedents, it is not surprising that Etruria was to play an important role in the last, confused months of the conspiracy.

But no slaves were welcome in Catiline's ranks. The rebellion Catiline was planning through the second half of 63 BC was a restricted club: Roman citizens only, thank you. Slaves might have provided him with many able fighters, people who, given their station in life, in effect had nothing to lose. But he kept them out, and the reason is evident.

Catiline was a Roman aristocrat: he had never promised freedom to the slaves, had no intention of granting it, and did not feel he could ask them to shed blood for a cause in which they would fundamentally remain in the same conditions as before. If that seems too good to be credible, we can turn it around (it amounts to the same result): Catiline did not want to be confused with Spartacus, whose bloodied, brutal rebellion had been crushed only ten years earlier. Spartacus had fought against Rome. Catiline was fighting *for* Rome against the mucilaginous, corrupt, double-crossing politics of his day. He was fighting for the Rome of old, which he had never seen but which had been passed down to him as an almost sacred memory, defining the duties of a man of his class. Catiline's revolution was designed in a conservative direction, or as one historian put it, an "archaic" revolution.

Slaves could not, should not, be part of this fight: it was a struggle of Romans against Romans, and at stake to him was the moral regeneration of the city. The best parallel from modern times probably is the German officers who, at great personal risk, tried to kill Adolf Hitler on July 20, 1944: they were fighting for the moral integrity of Germany just as much as Catiline was fighting for the moral integrity of Rome two thousand years earlier. There was no room in his fight for slaves, just as there would not have been room in the Germans' fight for a Russian or an American. Some actions you can either do alone or you cannot do them at all.

Even without slaves, it was a motley crew: rich and poor, young and old, farmers and urbanites, senators and workers, men and (astonishingly) women, Etruscans and Gauls, Greeks and Umbrians, desperate folks and well-heeled youths. The variety of people that attended his planning meetings speaks of a widespread thirst for social and political change.

In that fall of 63 BC, after Cicero's appalling dishonesty in pushing back the election date had convinced Catiline that there could be no progress or accommodation with the existing power élite, the very diversity of his supporters allowed him to start laying out the operational side of the uprising. Arms were dispatched and hidden in different areas of Italia. Commanders appointed, a relay system of messengers was organized, money—always necessary in cases like this—was stashed away in different places. The one problem Catiline did not have to worry about was food: an army may march on its stomach, as a certain Corsican said, but summer 63 BC had shown that he could count on an unprecedented level of support throughout the countryside. The farmers whose vote had been denied by Cicero's chicanery would feed them. The whole of Italia seemed ready and waiting for the signal to start.*

Eventually, the signal came.

But from the wrong side.

One of the people involved in the organization was named Quintus Curius. He had been a senator but had been expelled on Pompey's request in 70 BC, his fault being that he had blown a considerable patrimony gambling, which brought the Senate into disrepute and made him thereby "unworthy." By this time, Curius was not in his prime, but he insisted on keeping a mistress, a woman named Fulvia, about whom we know little, though it appears she was considerably younger than him. Between one steamy sex session and another, Curius, probably to impress his lover, started to talk: arms were being sent, troops were being trained, money was being hidden. Fulvia was no fool and realized that this kind of pillow talk was worth gold. She milked Curius mercilessly, demanding details, places, dates, locations, and, most importantly, names. Gaius Manlius had been detailed to Etruria; Septimius to Picenum; Gaius Julius to Apulia; Gaius Marcellus to Capua

---

*Allen argues that 63 BC saw a tightening of the credit conditions in Rome, which increased interest rates and with that raised the burden on the indebted poor. This attracted new recruits to the revolt. The argument is intriguing, but the notion of higher interest rates is only speculative. Allen's argument is based on evidence that gold was being exported from Rome, which would indeed increase interest rates, so it is plausible.

(Spartacus's old training school); others to Umbria, Gallia Cisalpina, Latium, Aretium, Africa. Fulvia must have had a fantastic memory.

On the evening of September 23, 63 BC, Fulvia knocked on the door of a well-appointed house in the center of Rome. Strange though it was for a woman to be out on her own as darkness fell, she was admitted, and the master of the house was summoned. The man who appeared before her had a narrow chest and a stooped back. But he was a consul of the republic, the best-known lawyer in the city. Fulvia began to spill the beans, and Cicero did not take long to understand how lucky he was. Fulvia had given him all he needed. Or almost.

Cicero had already heard that secret meetings were taking place in the city. His source was Caesar, whose ears were always close to the ground among the populares. Fulvia's information confirmed Caesar's but left Cicero in an infuriatingly constrained position. He could not move against Catiline and his lot because they would have laughed at him and explained the whole thing away as the inventions of Curius's old brain. Where exactly are the arms, consul? The money? Oh you don't know! Well, then, the evidence is somewhat lacking, is it not?

In principle Cicero had two options. He could organize a military counterstrike and catch them before they were ready, or he could have them arrested and dragged before the courts on charges of sedition, and then a nice death sentence could be handed down. But on mature reflection, neither would work, because if he was going to make a compelling argument and support it with evidence, he would have to reveal his sources. Caesar would never come forward—he had too many friends in the ranks of the conspirators and was in general too careful or opportunistic to expose himself. Fulvia had "cheap slut" written all over her. Can you imagine what that pain in the neck, Cato, would have said seeing her as chief witness for the prosecution? And in any event, Fulvia could only report what she knew second hand and would have had to point the finger at Curius.

Even so, a conviction of the conspirators could have been secured, as Murena's absolution had. But there is a big difference between a conviction and a death sentence: if these people got out of jail at some point, Cicero's life would be at a nasty end. And in any event, either a death sentence or a conviction would have caused certain consequences in public order: demonstrations, riots, attempted coups. In fact, a legal attack may have been just the event Catiline was waiting for to strike. Feelings over the summer's caper with the election dates still ran high. Revolts could be expected. And the object of these revolts was going to be Cicero. It's no wonder he started walking around Rome wearing a military breastplate, which on his sickly frame made him look somewhat ludicrous.

Beside these worrying considerations, Cicero came under a great deal of domestic pressure from his wife, Terentia, whose sister was the vestal virgin rumored to have yielded to Catiline. Terentia wanted Cicero to go after Catiline by any means necessary, exact revenge, and close the matter once and for all. For about a month, Cicero hesitated. We do not know who else he told of Fulvia's visit—it probably would have been difficult to hide it from Terentia, of course—but he does not seem to have discussed the matter with others. Caesar did not want to know, though he probably knew everything Cicero did and more. Crassus was a political opponent even if he had defended Murena side by side with Cicero; Crassus could easily turn the situation to his own advantage, for example, raising another army and going after Catiline as he had done with Spartacus. The aristocracy would have treated Cicero with contempt: unsubstantiated rumors, bedroom gossip from that old crook Curius. At a loss, all Cicero could think of was to call an extraordinary meeting of the Senate where he hinted darkly that there were moves afoot, naming no names (he couldn't). The senators appear to have been less than impressed.

But someone was beginning to worry about the time this was taking, someone who had access to the same information as Fulvia had given Cicero, and possibly more. On October 20, while the consul still sat on his hands and mused about what to do, there came a new knock on his door. The visitor this time was Crassus, accompanied by two other senators. Crassus was bearing gifts: a bundle of letters, still sealed in their envelopes, addressed to a number of senators. The letters, he explained, had been delivered earlier that evening to his servants by an unknown man who had disappeared in the shadows of the night (a likely story). Crassus had opened only the envelope addressed to him. The letter inside bore no signature but warned him that he should leave Rome as quickly as possible because someone was planning to massacre the senators in the next few days. Did the consul, Crassus asked, want to open the other envelopes?

Cicero did not. Like the good lawyer he was, he feared that someone would accuse him of tampering with the evidence. He had Crassus leave the bundle with him, and the next morning he called a second extraordinary meeting of the Senate for the following day, October 22. We can imagine that some senators rolled their eyes at the summons ("Oh, ye gods, here goes that Cicero again!"), while Crassus and a few others were sharing a goblet of wine to the success of their plan.

Cicero's stage management on October 22 was a masterpiece. He arrived with a slave bearing the bundle of sealed envelopes and delivered them right there in the Senate chamber to each addressee, calling out their names one by one. In the perfect silence that followed, he asked each senator in turn to open his envelope and read aloud the letter inside it. One by one the senators did, and each letter said pretty well the same: get out of Rome while you can because a bunch of conspirators intend to kill you. As each stunned senator's voice rang out in the silence, Cicero stood in the middle of the floor, in the place reserved for speakers. These theatrics made an immense impression on the senators. Coming so soon after Cicero's dark hints of a few weeks earlier, this provided irrefutable evidence that the Senate, the republic, Rome itself, stood in the gravest danger. They were all on the brink of a new civil war, one planned with cool determination and ferocity.

The Senate immediately approved an emergency law that gave Cicero and Hybrida full powers. Police escorts were ordered for public officials. Street patrols were increased. Gates, crossroads, and squares were monitored by heavily armed troops. Cicero could have ordered the arrest of the people Fulvia had told him about, but he waited. It may be that he did not really trust her and Curius. It may also be that he wanted to force the conspirators' hand and draw them out into the open.

On October 24, a magistrate from Etruria got up to speak in the Senate. He said he had received a letter from Faesulae (modern-day Fiesole, near Florence), and he read it in the chamber. The letter informed him that on October 27, centurion Gaius Manlius would start the armed revolt.* The Senate voted to send General Quintus Marcius Rex to face Manlius and General Quintus Metellus Creticus to Apulia, in order to monitor what was happening in the south. Both generals had just returned after successful campaigns, so their armies were in full operational mode. Praetores were sent to different provinces to enlist all the men they could, and as a precaution that tells us what a trauma Rome had experienced with Spartacus's revolt, the gladiator schools were shut down and their charges redistributed across different cities and provinces. That this conspiracy was a very different matter from Spartacus's did not seem to cross the senators' minds.

In any event, the letter about Manlius was the blow that exposed the conspiracy: after the other letters, it was credible in a way that Fulvia could never be. At the end of October 63 BC, Rome's security apparatus was gearing up. In a move that many modern law enforcement

---

*A centurion was the commander of a unit of the Roman army usually made up of one hundred men, though the number could vary depending on circumstances. The unit was called a centuria and formed the basic voting unit of the Comitia Centuriata.

agencies would recognize, cash prizes and immunity from prosecution were offered to those who broke ranks with the conspiracy and came clean. If they were slaves, they were to be freed.

This last measure shows yet again how far the Roman establishment was from understanding what was happening in fall 63 BC: it was fixated on Spartacus. Catiline's initiative was more difficult to come to terms with, as it involved a reshaping of Roman society and its institutions, not just indiscriminate sacking and murdering. But sacking and murdering was what the senators thought about.

Once the letter about Manlius was made public, the game was in the open, and the leader of this outrageous initiative was well identified. The Senate had Catiline charged with the crime of public violence (*de vi*), in effect the crime of inciting, preparing, or carrying out an attack against the government, its agencies, or its officials. By that law, anyone charged could be arrested without a specific warrant.

At this point, Catiline decided to play the game and up the ante. He invoked an old custom that allowed anyone charged with a crime to give himself up to a "notable citizen" who would keep him in his house until a trial could begin. The custom was similar to what happens today when a person is released into the custody of a third party who guarantees the whereabouts of the accused. By not giving himself up to the judicial authority, the person being accused openly denied that there were any grounds for the charges against him. At the same time, he guaranteed that he would remain at the disposal of the authorities by residing with someone whose reputation excluded a possible collusion and escape. In an economy where credit was scarce and raising cash difficult, this also meant the accused did not have to try to raise bail.

In this way, Catiline showed his respect for the law while remaining reasonably free to act. What he does not seem to have done is wondered how the information contained in the letters had gotten out. If he had, he might have asked who of his small circle knew enough about the conspiracy to pass on a sense of immediate threat to the consul. Among his associates, for what we know, only one had a rather checkered career, having lost a fortune in gambling, been expelled from the Senate, and spent what little money he had left on young girlfriends of doubtful repute, and having a reputation as a blabbermouth. None of these necessarily proved Curius was the source of the leak, but it created a whiff of doubt if nothing else. A forceful interrogation would likely have produced some revelations from Curius, and then that channel could have been either blocked or used to provide misinformation to Cicero.

Catiline does not seem to have seen things that way. The first notable citizen he chose to give himself up to in the matter of the accusation of "public violence" was Senator Marcus Aemilius Lepidus, whose wife was Junia, the sister of Marcus Junius Brutus, Sempronia's husband. But Lepidus turned him down, and we do not know why.

Catiline then chose another prominent citizen to host him. He went and knocked on the same door that Fulvia and Crassus had: let the consul himself keep him in his house. The mockery was open and merciless.

It is not clear whether Cicero had been expecting him. But the fact remains that the door was bolted and barricaded when Catiline arrived. Voices were heard from the inside, insults and threats uttered by Cicero's servants against Catiline. In the end, Catiline gave it up as not worth pursuing and retreated to a friend's house—possibly that of a fellow conspirator. He was still running the plot, but it is worth stressing again that he does not seem to have thought about where the consul was getting his information, or, if he did, he did not identify Curius. In reality, the older man was by then completely controlled by Fulvia, who was being paid by the police. She threatened to expose him. Naturally, he talked. She reported to Cicero.

Meanwhile, the Senate had decreed that extra wheat should be distributed. This was a simple but reliable way to buy off the poor and pull the rug from under Catiline's feet. *Panem et circenses*: bread and circuses.

In addition, the optimates may also have started a rumor that the conspirators had been planning to set Rome on fire. This was the purest nonsense, but it fed on the poor's unrestrained terror of fire. For all its empire, most of Rome consisted of ramshackle wooden structures leaning against each other. A spark was enough to start off a general conflagration. Without high-pressure water mains, dousing it was close to impossible. As a defensive political strategy the rumor was effective and allowed the consuls to place more heavily armed troops all over the city, along the roads, by the gates, in the Forum, on the bridges.

This kind of police-military presence had a psychological impact on the conspirators. Attractive though it may have been to prepare for a just and noble war, the sight of seriously armed, experienced soldiers around every corner could not fail to drive home the point that the odds were not in the plotters' favor. The only event that would compensate for the government men's experience and weaponry was a mass uprising guided by a hardcore fighting party made up of the conspirators. Without pushing the analogy too far, this is the problem faced by all would-be leaders of a coup d'état: you need a mass on your side to overwhelm the defenders of the established order. But in that mass there must be a few trained individuals to strike at the nerve points of power. Leon Trotsky might have given Catiline a few valuable lessons. The first would probably have been: find the spies and kill them. There is always at least one.

At the end of the first week of December, Catiline gathered his closest staff in the house of Senator Marcus Porcius Laeca. Among those present were Lentulus, Cethegus, Statilius, Gabinius, Vergunteius, and Curius. Catiline might as well have had Cicero himself there. Faced with the evidence that the conspiracy was known and they were in serious danger, they decided to take a dramatic initiative. In the morning, two of them (Vergunteius and Gaius Cornelius) would attend Cicero's open house where friends and supporters came to ask for assistance, and kill the consul. The murder was to be the signal of the revolt: Lentulus and Cethegus were to take over the communication, command, and control points of Rome, while Catiline was to leave at full speed to meet Manlius in Etruria and march back down. They were to relieve Cethegus and Lentulus, while also reinforcing their position in Rome before the generals

Marcius and Metellus had time to turn around and provide support to the troops left in the city. It was time to move. Quickly.

Vergunteius and Cornelius walked to Cicero's house in the morning, their daggers under their cloaks, and (oh, what a revelation!) found the door barricaded again. Again, voices from inside were heard shouting abuse. The two would-be assassins gave it up: obviously they were known, their game was over. The death penalty awaited them. Their only hope was to run away from Rome, which they did.

Cicero called a new Senate meeting for November 8. He had the army surround the building. It was not the usual Senate building. Instead it was the Temple of Jupiter in the Forum, as if the consul had wanted to call upon himself the protection of the father of the gods. Incredibly, Catiline was still playing innocent and went to the meeting.

As he sat on his bench, all other senators moved away from him, including people who had attended his meeting in the house of Senator Marcus Porcius Laeca two days earlier. Those people certainly still supported him, but the fear was that by sitting with him they would in effect have denounced themselves: again, that they had already been identified by one of their own never seems to have crossed their minds.

In the silence that filled the temple, Cicero stood up. It must have taken a great deal of pluck for this man, who was not naturally brave, to walk to the center of the floor, his steps echoing over those few paces. Then in the silence of the Senate, he turned to face Catiline and exploded in one of the most powerful opening lines of all times:

"Quo usque tandem abutere, Catilina, patientia nostra? Quam diu etiam furor iste tuus nos eludet? Quem ad finem sese effrenata iactabit audacia?"

"Just how long will you take advantage of our tolerance, Catiline? And for how long will that madness of yours laugh at us? Where do you think you are going to get to?"

Imagine these words being spoken with a measured rage, and feel their aggressive weight, their threat and their derision. The message is, "I know all there is to know, so what are you still doing here?" Imagine then sitting at your place in the temple and being hit unexpectedly by this verbal assault. Before you could react, your sentence had already been set.

In the silence of the temple, the words echoed. Catiline, for all his bravery, must at first have been taken aback. But he was a tough guy and recovered quickly. He probably smiled at the words of this little, dishonest, provincial lawyer and sat back to enjoy the rest of the speech. But he knew he was playing with fire. The Senate had given Cicero the power to arrest him, when and where the consul chose. The consul had not yet exercised it, but the Temple of Jupiter was surrounded by heavily armed soldiers. This was martial law. All Cicero had to do was give a sign.

But Cicero did not give that sign. He just talked, and talked, and talked for more than two hours. That powerful opening was lost in a sea of words. Yes, Cicero built up indignation and heaped moral opprobrium on his rival. He told him to run away, to desist, to think about the terror he was spreading among the honest people of Rome, now that all was known and every street and city gate was guarded against him and his associates. At times the speech took on an almost pleading quality: please go away and stop terrorizing us. Just go.

Why Cicero did not arrest Catiline at the Senate session of November 8 remains unclear. He had all the evidence he wanted. At this point even Curius and Fulvia could have been paraded before a court; too much else was known for their dubious characters to damage what they said. But Cicero may have feared that an arrest carried out so openly would be counterproductive and spur the poor of the city to action. If so, he still had an inflated idea of the conspiracy's reach. This was probably given him by Fulvia, whose price, after all, would rise with the level of danger she would report.

Still, Cicero may have hoped that Catiline would take the hint and leave in a hurry. If that was Cicero's expectation, he had completely misread the psychology of his opponent. Catiline would stand and fight—as Cicero would not (and did not, at the crucial moment), so it may have been difficult for him to understand the mindset of the last of the Sergii.

But most likely, Cicero the lawyer stared at the legal problem confronting him. Assume he had Catiline arrested on November 8. Then what? Obviously he would have to be executed once convicted. The Senate could not take on the role of a court of justice in this case, so Catiline had to be judged for sedition and public violence by a regular court, and such courts were easy to pay off. Besides, Catiline was a Roman citizen, and Roman citizens condemned to death had the right to appeal to Comitia Centuriata. This was very dangerous: Cicero could not count on their decision, especially about a well-known and heroic military man. If, as Fulvia had reported, support for the conspirators was widespread, allowing Catiline to get to the centuriae was tantamount to setting him free again, and this time there would be no holding him back.

So Cicero spoke and spoke, probably to hide his own uncertainty and possibly, just possibly, to give Catiline the time to run away. For his part, Catiline listened, probably with scorn. After a while, bored by the rhetorical hollowness of Cicero's long-winded speech, he stood up, interrupted the consul, and spoke to the assembled Senate. He said only a few words (reported by Sallust), and their sense was this: he had shown in war his attachment to Rome. His family had built and nurtured the republic, and all of the Sergii had always followed the strictest rules of Roman conduct over centuries. It was laughable that his behavior should now be questioned by someone who had only just pitched his tent in Rome. This was a terrific slap on Cicero's face, who was posing as the defender of the city.

It backfired.

The Senate erupted. Catiline was called "enemy of the fatherland" and "child murderer." He spoke out at the howling aristocratic mob and repeated what he had told Cato not long before: "If any of you try to set a fire against me, I won't fight it with water, but with destruction." Then he turned and walked out. No senator or guard dared to hold him back.

But before we follow him, let's go back a minute: child murderer? Why child murderer? Catiline was married twice; he had a son from his first wife, and both wife and child died within a short time of each other (we do not even know their names). He then married Orestilla. But during his speech on November 8, Cicero inserted a despicably poisonous barb: "not a long time has passed," he had said, "since you freed up your house with the death of your first wife to welcome the second one. And did you not add another crime, an even worse one, to the first one? Ah, I had better not insist, I am happy to avoid talking about it, so that no one will know that in our city such a terrifying crime has been left unpunished."

Note that Cicero does not say it specifically, but the meaning of the passage makes it clear: the consul hinted that Catiline had, in order to marry Orestilla, murdered his first wife and then, since Orestilla did not like having the son around the house, murdered him. This was part of Cicero's construction of Catiline as an inhuman monster, ready to commit the most appalling crimes to satisfy a whim.

In Roman law, the murder of a close relative like a child was one of the few crimes that could be prosecuted directly by the officials of the state, without having to wait for charges to be laid by a private citizen. Cicero said "not a long time has passed" since the unspeakable crime took place. But even if we go back ten years from the date of the speech, there is no evidence of any prosecution against Catiline in those years, other than the ones we have already discussed. And in fact, Cicero did not say "you killed your wife and child." He hinted. He threw mud. He had no evidence, and none has surfaced in the two thousand years since.

But the mud has stuck.

11

THE MOVEMENT
UNRAVELS

CATILINE WALKED FREE OUT OF THE TEMPLE OF Jupiter, probably cursing. What was his next move? He could stay in Rome, where he could be arrested any minute. It would also mean abandoning Manlius's army to certain slaughter. Or he could move to Etruria, and there wait for the signal from the conspirators in Rome that they were ready. This would allow him to march down to the city, catching the government between two armies before the generals sent to Southern Italia had time to react. In all this, speed mattered: Catiline knew that Manlius's army was not large enough to hold the government troops for long. So Lentulus's revolt in the city itself had to start quickly in order to reduce the pressure on Manlius and on Catiline once he had joined up with the Etruscan contingent.

Catiline left Rome that night, accompanied by three young men as bodyguards and messengers. The move was clever: it made it seem as if Catiline was leaving Rome in acceptance of Cicero's orders. That bought him a few days before Cicero could pick up enough steam to get the government in Rome to move again, and in those few days Catiline would reach Manlius.

Before leaving, Catiline appointed Lentulus as his commander in chief in Rome. Lentulus was not an ideal choice: he came from the gens Cornelia, so his ancestors definitely ranked at the top of the aristocracy. But a sibylline prophecy had implied (or he thought it had) that he would be the third Cornelius to run Rome (there had already been two, Sulla and Cinna). With an unshakable faith in this nonsense, Lentulus decided he could replace Catiline, so that instead of following the orders given by Catiline, he started to do as he pleased. He began by recruiting slaves, something Catiline had forbidden, which lost the movement credibility with the Roman working classes and at the same time gave fuel to the aristocracy's accusations that this lot of maniacs were no more than a second edition of Spartacus. Those aristocrats who favored Catiline's initiative were dismayed, but the working class was more than dismayed, it was terrified. The feared arrival of hordes of slaves to fight in this revolt had only one meaning for them: it confirmed the rumors that had been going around about the plotters' intentions to set the city on fire. To the slaves, torching Rome would mean nothing; only a rebellion by poor people who lived side by side with each other in wooden huts could ensure that when the fighting died down there would still be a Rome. Lentulus obviously did not understand that and could not see why he had a great deal of trouble recruiting new people into the conspiracy.

Not happy with that, Lentulus prepared a plan that was, to say the least, insane. He had decided that the revolt would begin December 16, the day before the festival of the Saturnalia. This was a deeply important festival to the Romans, in honor of the god Saturn—an ancient agricultural divinity—during which for twenty-four hours usual social relations were reversed: masters waited on servants at the table, people masqueraded in the streets and donned unusual clothes, free banquets were held, and women directed the festivities. The world was turned, however briefly, upside down.

All of this may have had a symbolic logic to Lentulus's deluded brain. The idea was that the day before the Saturnalia, Lucius Calpurnius Bestia, a tribune, was to convoke the multitudes, speak to them of Cicero's iniquities, whip them up into a frenzy, and get them to murder the consul. Once he was out of the way, Lentulus and his friends would seize the control points of the city, kidnap Pompey's children so as to encourage him to keep out, and sit there. Lentulus had no intention of passing the command to Catiline.

Cethegus had many arguments with Lentulus. Why wait until the Saturnalia, almost a month away, and give the government troops time to prepare an attack on Manlius and Catiline? All that was needed was a few men to attack the Senate and arrest the senators, and that would be that. The city, the army, the police, would be paralyzed. Cethegus's plan may have been daring, but it could work. Lentulus said no.

But if the conspirators were dallying in November 63 BC, what was Cicero waiting for? He knew all their names, their plans, their locations. But he did not move. Why?

In part, the delay may reflect lawyerly caution: did he have all the papers signed, all the affidavits witnessed, all the documentation above all reproach? Not really. Then how could he begin bringing charges as serious as those he had in mind? And especially against people like that?

And that may have been the dominating concern. The conspirators came from the best families in Rome. Everyone among the *crème de la crème* of the aristocracy seemed to have a son or a nephew or a cousin involved. Moving against people of that sort was dangerous. If Cicero had brought charges, searched houses, arrested and put on trial these people, would there not in the future be someone else from the same gens who would seek revenge on this upstart provincial lawyer? These were not people to trifle with: happy to let him play the cat's-paw today, their unshakable solidarity as a class might well reveal itself too powerful for a former consul to resist.

Strangely, the Senate itself had given Cicero the solution. In the law that gave the two consuls full powers, the Senate had made a distinction, as was usual when calling up that piece of legislation. One consul was entrusted with controlling Rome itself: Cicero. Outside the city walls, the other consul took responsibility for managing emergency measures. In fall 63 BC, that other consul was Hybrida. The answer was perfect, provided Catiline would just clear out. Hybrida would have to go after him, and Cicero could rest, waiting for Catiline to be brought back as a prisoner. Then nobody could argue that Cicero had brought legal action against a member of their family without proper justification. Let Hybrida take the heat.

In November 63 BC, there came to Rome a delegation of Gauls from Provence to seek redress for the extortions that Murena (one of Sulla's generals in the fight against Mithridates) had subjected them to.* These people were known as the Allobroges, a fiercely independent tribal group with a fraught history in its relations with Rome: besides their habit of fighting against Roman envoys as the whim seized them, they appear to have been generally bellicose and bloody minded.† Julius Caesar, in his account of the civil war against Pompey, describes them as displaying "outstanding courage" in battle and relates that they had attacked Hannibal's much more numerous army as it crossed their territory on the way to the Alps in 217 BC. During the slaves' revolt of 73–71 BC, Spartacus's chief lieutenant, Crixus, had been an Allobrogian Gaul.

With that kind of résumé, one can understand Lentulus's desire to establish friendly relations with the Allobroges who were cooling their heels in the Forum waiting for the appropriate official to see them. Understand it but not approve of it, because these were people who would fight against Rome, not for it. Like slaves, they would have set the whole place on fire and

*Cicero, in *Pro Murena*, explains the background to this mission.
†The Allobrogian territory stretched along the east side of the Rhône River from the seashore around Nice all the way to Lake Leman. Geneva itself was an Allobrogian town.

thought no more about it. The conspiracy depended on keeping well clear of such people, but this was not self-evident to Lentulus.

Casual meetings were arranged, and Allobrogian complaints of Murena's iniquities respectfully listened to, probably with much head shaking. The Allobroges were wined and dined until someone suggested they might want to hear about the solution to their problem that was being discussed, right then, in Rome. They were invited to Sempronia's house, near the Forum (she appears to have been away at the time).

There they met Publius Gabinius Capito, who introduced himself as one of the leaders of the conspiracy. He explained to them what the plot was, how it would achieve its goals, and, in order to convince them that they were talking to someone who had responsibility, he appears to have given them names of other conspirators. The Allobroges listened politely, then said they'd need to talk about the whole idea and left.

Apparently the only benefit they could see for themselves and their tribe out of all that was to report their hosts to the Roman government and ask for a considerable reward.

So they did. They were quickly passed from one official up to the next until they managed to speak to Cicero himself. And Cicero recognized that the gods had sent him a second break. These were witnesses beyond all doubt. They had no axes to grind, no megalomaniac dreams, no past of corruptible behavior. They were straightforward, honest, untarnished warriors, and as a bonus they did not even like Rome very much. What could have driven them except telling the truth?

But they had to be used well. Cicero suggested they might want to go back to the strange gang that had so carelessly sought their help and ask to meet all conspirators' leaders and have them write letters explaining what they were up to and asking for the Allobroges' support. These letters, the ambassadors were to insist, would go back to the Allobroges' councils so their people would have the opportunity to discuss them. Cicero needed something signed, and this was one way to get it.

Amazing as it may seem, Cethegus, Lentulus, and Statilius accepted the Allobroges' request, wrote and signed the letters, and handed them over—apparently not realizing that their signatures constituted their death warrants. Only one of the conspirators, referred to in the histories only as Cassius, smelled a rat. He walked out of the meeting with the excuse he would leave for Gaul and speak directly to the Allobrogian chieftains. There is no record he ever got there, and for all we can tell he was lost to history.

The Allobroges left on December 2, escorted by some of the conspirators. They were to travel up to a port and from there embark for Provence. As they crossed the Milvian Bridge in the dark of the early evening, a Roman army troop sent by Cicero stopped them, "arrested" them, and took them back to the city. At dawn, they were brought to Cicero's house. He examined the letters that had been "found" in the Allobroges' possession and gave orders to send troops to arrest Lentulus, Cethegus, Gabinius, Statilius, and several others. The Allobrogian letters at long last gave him an irrefutable proof. He gave orders to call yet another extraordinary session of the Senate in the afternoon of December 3, this time to be held in the Temple of Concordia. Cicero walked there holding hands with Lentulus, as a sign of respect for the latter's office as praetor. Behind the two of them, surrounded by heavily armed men, came the other conspirators, the Allobrogian witnesses, and an army escort.

The temple was filled to bursting but nobody spoke. In the tense silence, Cicero organized another dramatic performance: he had the Allobrogian letters introduced as evidence. With them were brought into the temple the weapons that a search party had just found in Cethegus's house: swords, daggers, breastplates. Enough to fight a Roman army? Probably not, but there they were.

With this heap of weaponry on the floor before them, the members of the conspiracy, summoned one by one, lost their cool. Cicero pointed out to each of them that the Senate had granted immunity for those who helped. Knowing all too well what the alternative was, one by one they confessed.*

But confessed what, exactly? The Allobrogian letters were written in such anodyne terms that everything and nothing could be got out of them: "Those who bring to you this letter have reached with me an understanding that I hope you will honour, just as I will honour their understanding with us." What does that say? Nothing. We could be talking about fishing rights in the Rhône, the color of capes, the price of wine. One can imagine how these men, if they had been allowed to talk with their solicitors, could have defended themselves:

"But why, Cethegus, did you store all this weaponry in your home?"

---

*The events related to the Allobroges are discussed in March, "Cicero and the 'Gang of Five.'"

"My dear consul, I have always been an admirer of the fine art of weapon making. Look at the perfect edge of that steel blade, at the brilliant copper clasps on this belt, at the sheer perfection of the point of this spear, at . . ."

"Yes, yes, thank you."

Yet again, no incontrovertible evidence could be extracted. Letters, statements were ambiguous, unconvincing. But, noted Cicero, the behavior of these people was not. They hesitated, looked at the floor, exchanged furtive glances. It was as if just by being kept there they had lost a certain degree of self-assurance.

Then Lentulus had an idea. He asked the Allobroges to describe what they had talked about with him; even this late in the game, he appeared to view the Allobroges as friends and allies, not realizing they had been in cahoots with Cicero all along. To his dismay, the Allobroges confirmed the worst: they'd been asked to supply squadrons of cavalry to help the revolt, to travel to Faesulae and meet Catiline. They handed over a letter they were supposed to give to Catiline. The seal was Lentulus's. The contents confirmed the aims of the conspiracy. In the silence of the terrified Senate, wrote Cicero years later, Lentulus seemed to collapse in on himself.

By then the evidence was overwhelming: the conspirators had gone over the head of the Senate and established relations with a foreign power; they had been in contact with a man the Senate had declared a "public enemy"—Catiline; they had built up stashes of weapons and corresponded with a renegade fighting force that was approaching Rome. Each of these charges deserved the death penalty.

The effect on the poor of Rome was overwhelming. They still feared that there would be a fire in their streets and shops and homes. The people that were by now publicly linked to the conspiracy—slaves and foreigners—were perfectly capable of starting one in the city out of desire for revenge. What did they care?

Anyone who could stop them was therefore the protector of Rome, and Cicero was praised, applauded, cheered. He had delivered them from the fear of a burning death. Never mind that no evidence of setting a fire had emerged in the plotting of the conspirators. Never mind also that Cicero had told his friend and publisher Titus Pomponius Atticus that the story of the fire was a complete hoax to win popular support. Never mind Tabulae Novae or anything else: for an instant, the poor felt safe.

Catiline was far away, and his friends in Rome had been shamed before the Senate. The political mood had by then switched, in no small part thanks to Lentulus's strategic errors. When Cethegus's and Lentulus's servants tried to free their masters as they were being led from the temple, the crowd fought back and stopped them. Although he did not know it, that was the end of Catiline's dream. The poor had been lost.

12

THE SENTENCE

THERE WAS SOME HOLLOW VERBAL JOUSTING IN THE Senate on December 4, and on the following day the ultimate question presented itself to the senators in all its appalling majesty. It is easy to write that someone has to be condemned to death, however, when faced with the act, there is in most people some form of revulsion. But this may be a modern construct: the Romans certainly do not appear to have harbored much hesitation in the matter. Even so, the death penalty was always handled with great caution.

There was, in any event, no doubt in Cicero's mind. These were not, in his worldview, people who could somehow be redeemed and gently led back to their place in society. What evidence was gathered from the Allobroges and Cicero's own statements relating to what he knew from Fulvia, plus the radicalism of Catiline's speeches during the election campaign, had been so serious that the Senate—even though it was not, in law, a court—found them guilty of political crimes. Any offices these men had held were stripped from them: Lentulus himself had been forced to drop before the assembled Senate the purple toga of his praetorian office and put on a simple white one.

On December 5, ten weeks after Fulvia had first knocked on Cicero's door, the Senate met to discuss the penalty for the conspirators. Starting with the two consul designates, Silanus and Murena, both of whom argued for the "extreme penalty," one senator after another rose and asked that the conspirators be put to death. There were a few exceptions: a young senator named Tiberius Claudius Nero (who was to be the emperor Nero's adoptive grandfather) argued that not all facts had been laid out before the Senate, so it would be opportune to wait before pronouncing such an unforgivable penalty. Caesar argued that it was unwise to condemn Roman citizens to death. By law and custom, said Caesar, they had the right to appeal to the assemblies. This right of appeal, called *provocatio*, could not be ignored: the population of Rome would remember that the conspirators had been unable to appeal and would forget whatever they may have been guilty of. Better to let them live, confiscate their property, and exile them. That would be worse to them than executing them.

Caesar probably cared little about the lives of the conspirators. What mattered to him was to set the stage for a future attack on Cicero and possibly others. By preparing the argument that the law had been violated in this case by enforcing the death penalty on Roman citizens without giving them the right to file a provocatio, he was undermining Cicero.

Whatever his ultimate aim, that evening Caesar's idea had a certain appeal, and quite a few senators declared themselves in favor of it. Then Quintus Lutatius Catulus spoke. He was a friend of Catiline's, but he was also a conservative. He had always placed moral consistency above personal preferences, and did so this time too. The interests of the state, he declared, were the destruction of the plotters. Death was his vote. And it must have cost him emotionally because of his lifelong friendship with Catiline. Yet in taking this position, Catulus exhibited a personal steadiness that, if Catiline had been there, he might have appreciated.

Then it was Cato's turn. For once he got off his moral high horse and argued on purely practical grounds. It was not a matter of proving every last detail of a crime that had not yet been committed. That way lay destruction, for nothing that had not yet happened could be proven in its entirety. By the time you could prove it, the crime would have been committed, the government subverted, and then what would be the good of proving the crime? He was not talking about petty crimes but about grand designs that aimed to undermine the very essence of the rule embodied in public power. If public authority failed, there could only be merciless disorder, a war of all against all. Anyone wishing to damage public authority should, for the good of the common interest, be subject to the extreme penalty. He could only vote for death.

The meeting applauded his reasoning and cheered wildly. Caesar tried to intervene and have one of the tribunes veto the right of the Senate to hold a vote on imposing the death penalty on a Roman citizen, but was rebuffed.

So the death penalty it was. It was a victory for Cicero, but one he would eventually pay for dearly. In 58 BC, the tribune Publius Clodius Pulcher had a retroactive law passed that exiled magistrates and public officers who had condemned Roman citizens to death without allowing them to appeal to the assemblies. The law was specifically aimed at Cicero, and he had to accept it. He was exiled.

But on that evening of December 5, 63 BC, Cicero hurried to see the chief of police in Rome. The Senate had given him full power, and he was going to use it whether or not the people in jail at that moment had the right to a provocatio. Cato's speech had confirmed in his mind the importance of acting in exceptional circumstances without too strict an observance for the law, if the state required it.

The action was illegal and, in a moral sense, profoundly wrong: no one is guilty until proven so in a court of law; the principle was well understood by the Romans. The accused had a right to a proper trial with a legal defense—and who should know this better than Cicero himself. If a court condemned them, they still had the right to file a provocatio to the assembly of the centuriae. Both trial and appeal were being denied them, and it says a lot about their psychological collapse earlier that evening that none of them, as far as we know, protested the perfectly illegal action of the consul and insisted on their rights as a Roman citizen. The Senate was horrified by what had emerged, but there were voices that argued, like Caesar, in favor of their right to a proper trial and, if necessary, an appeal. Law and custom would have supported them.

It is easier to understand what Cicero did than to understand those who agreed with Caesar but did not argue their ideas. He wanted these men out of the way, in part to show his determination and in part for his old reason: he wanted to show he was more Roman than the Romans. He was the true protector of the city, the unwavering official who took it upon himself to punish these reprobates and bury them and their revolution forever. So he broke a few laws? Well, maybe, but it was only to protect a greater good. He was defending Rome against the mindless rage of the poor. Given the likely consequences of that, failing to respect the generous legal protection granted to criminals could not be seen as a serious matter. In fact, sticking to preordained legal rights that had been defined in earlier, safer times—that would be the real crime. It fell to him to take the terrible step. It fell to him to suspend de facto the legal guarantees that these men enjoyed and suspend them without discussion or voting. His was the responsibility, his was the heroic stance in the tragic moment. No trials, no appeals would stop him. He had a duty to Rome and he would carry it out. Cicero had evidently learned Sulla's lesson about doing whatever needed to be done. As always, there was probably good faith and self-serving convenience in this approach.

Modern analogies of his position are too numerous to count. How do you deal with terrorists? When can you break the law in the name of a greater good? When do you suspend legal guarantees and protections? When do you take the initiative and react, outside the law you are meant to protect, without a warrant? None of these are easy questions to answer. Cato that evening captured the essence of the political struggle in which we now live when he said that nothing that had not yet happened could be proven in its entirety. If the essence of a terrorist threat is that it cannot be proven, what tools remain for the protection of society? Threat, note, not action: terrorist actions can be investigated, and suspects indicted and tried, as with any other crime. The threat is more difficult to come to terms with, and the means by which it can be discovered, assessed, and countered are not necessarily legal. Even if he was acting in good faith, Cicero in that case pushed the limits of his authority too far, which forced him to spend the rest of his life blackening the reputation of the conspirators: the worse they were, the more his actions were justified. Politically, he soon paid for it. But for us, the questions remain.

That evening of December 5, 63 BC, Cicero summoned several people whose skills he needed. Under his orders, the condemned men were led from the places where they had been confined toward the Mamertine jail, at the back of the Capitoline Hill. Just to make the point yet again, these men were innocent: no court had passed a verdict on them, and the Senate had not constituted itself as a court in this case. In effect, no death penalty had been handed down, even if a majority of Senators had voted for death. But their votes meant nothing without a court to try the case, so Lentulus, Cethegus, and the others were, by law, innocent men. And provocatio was not being granted to them. But the Senate was exercising imperium and saw no real objection to its action.

Even if a sentence had been passed by a court in the presence of the accused men's counsel, they still had the right to appeal, which they had not been able to exercise. Whether or not one finds Catiline's ideas to be acceptable, what Cicero was doing that evening was not enforcing the death penalty on criminals. It was murder.

The accused and the Senate officials accompanying Cicero soon reached the Mamertine jail. This was an appalling place, a series of chambers dug deep into the side of the Capitoline Hill. Each level was made of stone flooring, supported by stone ramparts. There appear to have been no stairs, so that access to the execution chamber, some sixteen feet below street level, was only possible via a trapdoor through which the condemned men were lowered.

Cicero's prisoners were tied to a rod-and-tackle mechanism and lowered into the chamber, where the executioner waited. There, in the smelly darkness, their hands tied behind their backs, they were strangled.

Lentulus was first. Then Cethegus, Statilius, Gabinius, and the others. The corpses piled up in the death chamber under the dim light of the torches.

On the street, a small crowd had gathered. They were the families, the relatives, the friends of the men whom Cicero was having murdered in the jail. Someone—we do not know who—asked Cicero what was happening. The consul replied:

"*Vixerunt.*" They have lived.

The answer is appalling but, regrettably, grammatically correct. The word he used is the past perfect of the verb *vivere*, to live. The past perfect in Latin describes an action that has happened in the past and has now reached an end.

What Cicero did after this terrifying action is not known. He may have gone home followed by people cheering the deliverance of the fear of fire. He may have wondered if there were other conspirators who had escaped his net. He probably crossed the Forum on his way home.

By then, the sun had dropped below the violet horizon of the Tyrrhenian Sea, and in the morning it would be time to start shopping for presents to bring to friends for the upcoming Saturnalia. The last jars of olives were being brought to the Forum to be sold.

13

A PRIVATE
POSITION OF HONOR

W HEN CATILINE LEFT ROME, HE MUST HAVE KNOWN
his situation was desperate to the point of
death.* He was not afraid of death, but he knew that it
would mark the end of his dream of reshaping Rome
into the city it had been. Nobody behind him would be
able or willing to pick up his ideas, not Cato, not
Catulus, never mind the men he had had to leave behind
in charge of the few fighters he had been able to assem-
ble in the city. He rode on the Via Cassia, the road that
bent off the Via Flaminia after the Milvian Bridge and
reached northern Etruria and the mountain passes. From
some overnight stop he wrote a letter to Catulus. Catulus
had just voted for the death penalty for the conspirators,
but Catiline may not have known that. After Catiline

*This chapter relies on Sallust, *Bellum Catilinae*, 7.

was dead, the letter was introduced in the Senate, read aloud, and recorded. Sallust copied it in full, and there is great dignity in Catline's words. Here is the original:

L. Catilina Q. Catulo. Egregia tua fides re cognita, grata mihi magnis in meis periculis, fiduciam commendationi meae tribuit. Quam ob rem defensionem in novo consilio non statui parare; satisfactionem ex nulla conscientia de culpa proponere decrevi, quam, me dius fidius, veram licet cognoscas. Iniuriis contumeliisque concitatus, quod fructu laboris industriaeque meae privatus statum dignitatis non obtinebam, publicam miserorum causam pro mea consuetudine suscepi, non quin aes alienum meis nominibus ex possessionibus solvere non possem et alienis nominibus liberalitas Orestillae suis filiaeque copiis persolveret, sed quod non dignos homines honore honestatos videbam meque falsa suspicione alienatum esse sentiebam. Hoc nomine satis honestas pro meo casu spes reliquae dignitatis conservandae sum secutus. Plura cum scribere vellem, nuntiatum est vim mihi parari. Nunc Orestillam commendo tuaeque fidei trado; eam ab iniuria defendas per liberos tuos rogatus! Haveto!

Lucius Catilina to Quintus Catulus. I recognize your exceptional loyalty, a source of joy in this dangerous time, and it has again given me trust in my own abilities. I do not need to justify my current decision; and if I have chosen to account for it, it is not because of a feeling of guilt, God willing, it is appropriate that you should know the truth. Having suffered insults and injuries, because I was not able to enjoy the fruits of my labour and industry, or a private position of honour, I have taken up the public cause of the wretched, following my usual custom. I did so not because I am unable to pay the debts in my name with my own properties, and of course the generosity of Orestilla and her daughter has helped paying those in the names of others. But I did so because I saw shameless men raised to the highest honours while I was being kept away because of false suspicions about me. For this reason, hoping to preserve what dignity I still have, I am following this path. Considering my cause, it is honourable enough. I would like to write more, but an army is marching against me. Now all I can do is to beg you to take care of Orestilla, asking that you should protect her, and that you defend her from all attacks as if she was one of your own children. It is all I ask. Farewell!

Changing his route several times, Catiline picked up more men on his way to Faesulae. His group was carrying Marius's crest of gilded eagles, the symbols of Roman power under which Marius had defeated the Cymbri and Teutones all those years ago. The eagles were more than military insignia, they were the evidence of popular resistance to the abuses of the rich, embodied in the (much cleansed) memory of Marius. The ambiguity we can see nowadays was not apparent at the time, so let us accept these eagles as they were seen then.

Catiline had apparently kept Marius's insignia in his own home for years, possibly as war trophies captured when he was a young officer in Sulla's army. But as his ideas changed over the years, these old, gilded symbols took on a different value, and now that all bridges had been burned, he used them as a declaration of his identification with "the public cause of the wretched."

He was the real consul of the Roman republic.

Carrying Marius's eagles had another connotation: the eagles and their supports—long sticks with the symbolic representation of a bundle of rods bound together (the *fasces*)—were the signs of consular authority. Raising them at the head of an armed group meant challenging the very essence of Roman imperium. When the Senate found out about this new abuse of Catiline's, he was stripped of Roman citizenship. This was symbolic but also had powerful practical implications: killing Catiline was now not considered a crime.

Meanwhile, Hybrida had replaced Marcius Rex at the head of the Roman army that was marching north through Etruria. As Catiline rode up the Via Cassia with a handful of men, Hybrida, the consul in charge of dealing with rebellions outside of Rome, was approaching the valley of the Arno River (in today's terms, the area around Florence and Faesulae). His intention seems to have been to press Catiline's and Manlius's forces against the mountains north of Faesulae, blocking off their escape route that would connect them to the Via Aurelia and eventually, following the shore road, bring them to the plain of the Rhône in Provence.

After meeting up with Manlius's men, Catiline played cat and mouse with Hybrida's army. From late November through December, he moved almost without cease, marching west then north then south and never putting his small, ill-equipped force in a position where battle would be inevitable. The weather grew colder and supplies shrank. And still Catiline ran rings around the much more numerous army of Hybrida without engaging it.

Catiline was waiting for news from Rome. Yes, rebellions had started in other parts of Italia, but it was Rome that mattered. He could have moved west, crossed the Alps along the Via Aurelia and gone to hole up in Transalpine Gaul, where he could rebuild his army for the following spring.

But first he had to hear from Rome.

When he did, the news was appalling. Lentulus, Cethegus, and the others had been arrested, tried, and killed. The rebellion was over in the capital.

Meanwhile, the Senate, under Cicero's guide, had repeated its offer of immunity and cash to those who left the conspiracy by a certain date. As far as we know, none took it up. But the uprisings in other cities had been drowned in blood.

As Hybrida moved closer to Faesulae from the south, Quintus Metellus Celer brought his eighteen thousand men along the valley of the Po, on the northern slopes of the mountains. Catiline, on the southern slope and facing Hybrida's troops, had perhaps three thousand. He was now locked in; there was no escape.

Catiline could have crossed the mountains and delivered his men, exhausted after a journey over the steep terrain in very cold temperatures with hardly any food, into a meaningless battle. They would never even have gotten within striking range of the Roman army on the northern side: Metellus had excellent archers. Picking off the starving, half-frozen remnants of the crossing would have been no more than target practice.

So Catiline moved west and tried to reach the road that would connect him to the Via Aurelia along the seacoast. But at a town called Pistoia, some thirty-seven miles from the sea, he found Hybrida's vanguards. That was it: he could not continue without fighting.

We do not know how large Hybrida's army was, but it must have been several times Catiline's. When the two armies met, the new year had just started: it was the year in which, but for Cicero's dishonesty, Catiline should have been starting his duties as consul, his "private position of honour."

The winter snow lay heavy on the sides of the mountains behind Catiline. He took up a position in a narrow valley, with steep sides to his right and left. Behind him the mountains provided a natural defense, at least for the time being. The valley was narrow at its entrance on the south, almost as if it were a funnel. His inferiority in numbers would in part be compensated by Hybrida's inability to spread out his forces.

He spoke to his men, but we have no firsthand record of what he said. Sallust, his enemy, claims that Catiline told his men not to go gently into the good night of death, but to fight with all they had, leaving behind them "a victory that would cost the enemy blood and tears." How Sallust could have known this is unclear since, by his own assertion, no one who heard the speech survived to relate it, but his account may reflect a grudging admiration for Catiline's courage.

Then Catiline dismounted his horse and chased it away. He would fight as a Roman aristocrat, on foot, among his men.

In a sullen dawn on January 5, 62 BC, the two armies faced each other. Hybrida's men threw their javelins and spears in typical Roman military style, but in that narrow valley both weapons were quickly discarded. The whole battle took place at very close quarters in a frantic sword fight. The rebels resisted for a while, but the government troops were too numerous: they broke through Catiline's wings and in effect surrounded his army. Manlius was killed and so was the other wing commander, known only as Faesulanus ("the man from Faesulae"). Soon it became a massacre.

As far as we know, there were no survivors among Catiline's men. Government troops counted three thousand dead rebels. Sallust wrote that "after the battle, you could tell how much daring and energy Catiline's troops had displayed." Nobody had run away, nobody was found with a wound on his back. They had all died where they fought, facing the enemy.

The Roman army had suffered heavily, though no exact figures are known. "The best fighters," again according to Sallust, "had died in the fighting or had suffered terrible wounds."

Lucius Sergius Catilina was found a short distance away from the corpses of his men, among the bodies of the government soldiers he had slain. His face still displayed the expression of haughty defiance he had carried in life. He was still breathing, but he died shortly after being found.

Epilogue

According to Cicero, Catiline's body was taken back to Rome and cremated, as aristocrats traditionally were.

But farther up the mountain from where the final battle took place, at around 2,230 feet above sea level, there is a small town of some one thousand six hundred people called Cutigliano. The town's name may derive from Catilianum—"Catiline's town"—suggesting a town founded by survivors of the final battle. These were not necessarily fighting men but (if Sallust was right) the camp followers of the rebel army: wives, girlfriends, children, young males, possibly servants. The local city council does not officially endorse this etymology, but that has not stopped the town from naming the central plaza Piazza Catilina, "Catiline Square."

It is, as far as I know, the only public space in the world named after Catiline.

NOTES

p. xv: "Rome's wealthiest man." (Plutarch, "The Life of Crassus," in *Fall of the Roman Republic*, 8. For a biography of Spartacus, see Trow.)

p. xv: "The most splendid fellow." (De Ste. Croix, 25)

p. xvi: "Lt. Spartacus." ("Airliner Hijacker Returns to U.S. after 30 Years," *Time*, November 6, 2013; CBS/AP News, "Hijacker William Potts Faces US Judge after Return from Cuba," November 7, 2013.)

p. xx: "Endure hunger, cold, and want of sleep." (Sallust, 1, 5.2–6; Pareti, 332–335)

p. 2: "Fifty thousand people." (Scullard, *History*, 316)

p. 5: "Twenty years before Catiline's birth." (Scullard, *Gracchi*, 75–82)

p. 6: "As Marius ran for consul." (Zullino, 25–29)

p. 18: "In unclear circumstances." (Scullard, *Gracchi*, 35–36)

p. 28: "Had a powerful intellect." (Sallust, 1, 5.1–5.2)

p. 39: "The accounts speak." (Plutarch, *Life of Sulla*, 29.4)

p. 40: "That commander was." (Ibid.; Fini, 17)

p. 45: "Sulla now began." (Plutarch, *Life of Caesar*, 1)

p. 45: "Ancient authors talk." (Appian, 1, 103; Fini, 22n30; Mommsen, 106)

p. 45: "As Sulla scratched the name out." (Suetonius, 1; Plutarch, *Caesar*, 1)

p. 48: "Catiline enticed Gratidianus." (Cicero, *In toga candida*, cited in Puccioni, 29; Plutarch, *Sulla*, 32)

p. 50: "It turns out to have been related." (Cicero, *In toga candida,* fragments 2, 9, 10, and 16, in Puccioni, 26–41)

p. 57 "A legionnaire's annual salary." (Grant, 43–44)

p. 62: "Asconius, who relates this story." (Cicero, *In toga candida,* in Puccioni, 29–35)

p. 62: "Fabia was acquitted." (Cadoux, 166–167)

p. 63: "Together with Catiline." (Narducci)

p. 68: "In 88 BC." (Plutarch, *Life of Cicero*, 3, 2)

p. 69: "In Greece he worked with." (Haskell, 75–78)

p. 72: "He introduced into Latin." (Conte, 199)

p. 73: "You couldn't go to the Senate." (Plutarch, *Cicero*, 3)

p. 76: "There is some suspicion." (Fini, 48; Zullino, 69)

p. 78: "I am thinking I might." (Cicero, *Ad Atticum*, 1, 2, 1, in Carcopino, *Cicero,* 73–74)

p. 81: "The lawsuit, however ridiculous." (Narducci)

p. 82: "The only one who." (Pareti, 339–340)

p. 83: "Haughty defiance." (Cicero, *Pro Murena*, 51; Sallust, 61, 9)

p. 83: "Said what he thought." (Fini, 62)

p. 89: "We know who attended the meeting." (Phillips, 441–442)

p. 94: "The agreement was that Catiline." (Fini, 69–70)

p. 95: "Crassus called a new meeting." (Sallust, 18, 8. Strangely, only Sallust describes this second attempt.)

p. 99: "In the Roman Republic." (Cicero, *Pro Murena*, 50)

p. 101: "In reality, Hybrida had." (Pliny, 213)

p. 104: *"Publicam miserorum."* (Sallust, 35)

p. 104: "Wanted to change." (Dio Cassius, bk. 37, 50, 41–42; Plutarch, *Cicero*, 10, 11)

p. 108: "These were immense powers." (Fini, 56–58)

p. 109: "He had been Catiline's friend." (Zullino, 99)

p. 110: "The bill aroused the fury." (Fini, 81)

p. 110: "This man was." (Ibid., 78–81; Zullino, 78–85)

p. 111: "In the hot summer of 63 BC." (Sallust, 27)

p. 112: "If any of you." (Cicero, *Pro Murena*, 51)

p. 114: "Once, this landed him." (Plutarch, *Life of Cato*, 5)

p. 121: "From all this." (Syme, 25)

p. 121: "Still another social group." (Fini, 93–94; Zullino, 109–111)

p. 123: "No better than a prostitute." (Cicero, *In Catilinam* 2, 7)

p. 123: "Some Roman writers." (Zullino, 101)

p. 124: "An 'archaic' revolution." (Allen, 78, 82–83)

p. 126: "By this time." (Schweers, 8–10; Sallust, 23, 3)

p. 133: "Among his associates." (Fini, 94–95)

p. 137: *"Quo usque tandem."* (Cicero, *In Catilinam*, 1; my translation)

p. 140: "Not a long time has passed." (Ibid., 15; Zullino, 134–135)

p. 145: "Julius Caesar, in his account." (Caesar, ch. 39)

p. 145: "During the slaves' revolt." (Appian, 1, 116. See Carsana for background information on the Allobroges.)

p. 147: "Only one of the conspirators." (Cicero, *Pro Sulla*; Pareti, 414–415)

p. 148: "He gave orders to call." (March, 230–233)

p. 148: "Those who bring to you." (Cicero, *In Catilinam*, 3, 20)

p. 149: "In the silence." (Ibid., 3.2; Sallust, 40–45; Plutarch, *Cicero*, 18.4)

p. 150: "Never mind also that Cicero." (Fini, 120)

p. 164: "A victory that would cost." (Sallust, 59, 5)

p. 165: "After the battle." (Ibid.)

p. 165: "The best fighters." (Ibid., 61, 9)

p. 165: "He was still breathing." (Ibid.)

BIBLIOGRAPHY

THIS IS A PARTIAL BIBLIOGRAPHY, REPORTING THE works I found most useful in writing this book. It covers first ancient authors, then modern scholarly works, and last interesting works of fiction.

ANCIENT AUTHORS

Appian of Alexandria. *Historia Romana.*

Caesar, Gaius Julius. *De Bello Civili.*

Cicero, Marcus Tullius. *In Catilinam.* Cicero's speeches. Brilliant but so long-winded you want to scream.

———. *Pro Caelio.*

———. *Pro Murena.*

———. *Pro Sulla.*

Dio Cassius. *Historia Romana.*

Pliny (Gaius Plinius Secundus). *Naturalis Historia,* ch. 8.

Plutarch (Lucius Mestrius Plutarchus). *Parallel Lives.* This includes several biographical works—including those of the Gracchus brothers, Marius, Sulla,

Sertorius, Caesar, Pompey, Crassus, and Cicero—that provide information directly or indirectly on Catiline and his period. Beautifully written, although his insistence that physical appearance reflects moral character is grating to a modern mind-set.

Quintus Asconius Pedianus. *Sankt Gallen Manuscript Orationum Ciceronis Quinque Enarratio.* The original manuscript has been lost; all that remains is the version copied by hand in 1416 by Gian Francesco Poggio Bracciolini, currently kept in Madrid.

Quintus Tullius Cicero. *Commentariolum Petitionis.*

Sallust (Gaius Sallustius Crispus). *Bellum Catilinae.* This is the work to read before all others. It gives an overall view of the context, in spite of its obvious bias.

Suetonius (Gaius Suetonius Tranquillus). *De vita Caesarum.*

MODERN AUTHORS

A complete bibliography on Catiline would fill many pages, and I am not going to attempt it. One researcher counted almost one thousand titles (see Nicola Criniti, *Bibliografia Catilinaria,* Milan: Università Cattolica, 1971). Anyone interested in Catiline would do well to read Criniti's work, which usefully separates credible historical publications from fictional stories.

Allen, Walter. "In Defence of Catiline." *Classical Journal* 34 (1938): 70–85. A must.

Cadoux, T. J. "Catiline and the Vestal Virgins." *Historia: Zeitschrift für Alte Geschichte* 54, no. 2 (2005): 162–179. The vestal trial in all its silliness.

Carcopino, Jérôme. *Cicero: The Secrets of His Correspondence.* New York: Routledge & Kegan Paul,

1951. A biased account by a clear-minded author. Well worth reading.

———. *Les Etapes de l'impérialisme romain*. Paris: Hachette, 1961. Great on context.

Carsana, Chiara, ed. *Commento storico al libro II delle Guerre Civili di Appiano*. Pisa: Edizioni ETS, 2007.

Conte, G. B. *Latin Literature: A History*. Baltimore: Johns Hopkins University Press, 1999.

De Ste. Croix, Geoffrey. *The Class Struggle in the Ancient Greek World*. Ithaca, NY: Cornell University Press, 1989.

Fini, Massimo. *Catilina: Ritratto di un uomo in rivolta*. Milan: Mondadori, 1996. Great fun: an irreverent journalist slays a few sacred cows.

Grant, Michael. *Tacitus: The Annals of Imperial Rome*. London: Penguin Classics, 1996.

Haskell, H. J. *This Was Cicero*. New York: Alfred A. Knopf, 1900. Thorough—and pedantic.

Keegan, John. *A History of Warfare*. Toronto: Key Porter, 1993. A fascinating tour de force by a leading contemporary historian of warfare. If you want to find out what it was like to be a Roman legionary in battle, this is the book. Read chapter 4.

March, Duane A. "Cicero and the 'Gang of Five.'" *Classical World* 82 (1989): 225–234. The whys and wherefores of the Senate "trial" of December 3, 63 BC.

Mommsen, C. M. Theodor. *Römische Geschichte*. 3 vols. Leipzig, Germany: Reimer & Hirsel, 1854–1856. Thorough, careful, complete. A work of extraordinary scholarship in a grand tradition as few can manage to produce today. Not, however, an easy read.

Narducci, B. *Processi politici nella Roma antica.* Bari, Italy: Laterza, 1995. A dispassionate look at what it was like to be hit by trumped-up lawsuits in ancient Rome.

Netti, J. P. *Rosa Luxemburg.* London: Oxford University Press, 1969.

Pareti, L. "Catilina." *Studi minori di storia antica.* Vol. 3. Naples: D'Auria, 1965. A lot of information packed into a few pages.

Phillips, E. J. "Catiline's Conspiracy." *Historia: Zeitschrift für Alte Geschichte* 25, no. 4 (1976): 441–448. A thoughtful modern reassessment.

Puccioni, Giulio. *M. Tulli Ciceronis Orationum Deperditarum Fragmenta.* Florence: Mondadori, 1972. Fragments 2, 9, 10, and 16 of Cicero's *In toga candida* are the crucial ones for our story.

Rostovtzeff, Mikhail Ivanovich. *Social and Economic History of the Roman Empire.* New York: Biblo & Tannen, 1926. Another great scholarly work.

Schweers, Anja. "Frauen- und Männerbilder im alten Rom." In *Der altsprachliche Unterricht.* Vol. 42, no. 2. Hannover, Germany: Friedrich Verlag GmbH, 1999.

Scullard, Howard H. *From the Gracchi to Nero: A History of Rome, 133 BC to AD 68.* London: Routledge, 2010.

———. *A History of the Roman World, 753 to 146 BC.* London: Routledge, 2002. Very good on background for our story.

Syme, Ronald. *Sallust.* Berkeley: University of California Press, 1964. If you want a brilliant portrait of Catiline's enemy, this is the place to go.

Tatum, W. Jeffrey. *The Patrician Tribune: Publius Clodius Pulcher.* Chapel Hill: University of North Carolina Press, 1999.

Trow, M. J. *Spartacus: The Myth and the Man.* Stroud, UK: Sutton, 2006.

Vervaet, Frederik Juliaan. "The 'Lex Valeria' and Sulla's Empowerment as Dictator (82–79 BC)." *Cahiers de l'Institut Gustave Gloïz* 15 (2004): 37–84.

Zullino, Pietro. *Catilina; L'inventore del colpo di stato.* Milan: Rizzoli, 1985. Fanciful but fun.

WORKS OF FICTION

Two important playwrights have written tragedies about Catiline. Ben Jonson (1572–1637), English Jacobean playwright, wrote *Catiline His Conspiracy* in 1611. Henrik Johan Ibsen (1828–1906), Norwegian dramatist, wrote *Catiline,* his first play, in 1850. Both Jonson and Ibsen have rather imaginative love interests mixed in with their plots. The works are not often performed today.

Antonio Salieri (1750–1825), director of the Italian opera at the Habsburg court in Vienna, wrote an opera in two acts on the subject of Catiline's conspiracy, *Catilina* (libretto by G. Casti). Written in 1792, it has a very unlikely plot involving a love affair between Catiline and a daughter of Cicero's. The timing was not conducive to success: with the French Revolution encouraging rebellion and social strife, and then the Restoration at the Congress of Vienna in 1815, any work with a Catilinarian political slant was unlikely to find favor with rich sponsors and aristocratic censors. As far as I am aware, the work has been performed only once, in 1994 at the Teatro Salieri in Legnago, near Verona, Italy. Legnago was Salieri's birthplace.

The two volumes of Henry William Herbert's *The Roman Traitor or the Days of Cicero, Cato and Catiline: A True Tale of the Republic* were published in 1853. The story is drawn almost exclusively from Cicero and Sallust, with embellishments.

The American author Steven Saylor has written the novel *Catilina's Riddle* (New York: St Martin's Press, 1993), a detective story in which a historically fictional sleuth associated with Cicero helps him unravel the intrigue organized by Catiline in 63 BC.

Catiline's conspiracy and Cicero's actions as consul play a large role in the novel *Caesar's Women* (Avon), by Colleen McCullough, as a part of her Masters of Rome series.

SPQR II: The Catiline Conspiracy (New York: St. Martin's Minotaur, 2001), by John Maddox Roberts, discusses Catiline's conspiracy from the perspective of a fictional senator named Decius.

Robert Harris's book *Imperium* (London: Hutchinson, 2006), based on Cicero's letters, covers the developing career of Cicero, with many references to his growing interactions with Catiline. The sequel, *Lustrum* (London: Hutchinson, 2009), published in North America as *Conspirata* (New York: Simon & Schuster, 2010), deals with the five years leading up to Catiline's conspiracy.

A Pillar of Iron (New York: Doubleday, 1965), by Taylor Caldwell, tells of the life of Cicero, especially in relation to Catiline and his conspiracy against Rome.

None of these works pretends to provide historical assessments: they just report Cicero's views with small modifications.

ACKNOWLEDGMENTS

THIS BOOK HAS GREATLY BENEFITTED FROM THE comments and criticism provided by Hella Bertrand and Bob Mercier. My copy editor, Ron Silverman, has done more to improve structure and flow than anyone could have asked for. Bruce H. Franklin of Westholme Publishing deserves exceptional thanks for having seen the potential of this text. Several librarians helped me greatly, especially the staff at the Seeley G. Mudd Library at Yale University, and the staff at the Biblioteca Nazionale Centrale in Florence, where I am especially indebted to Alessandro Sardelli. My grade 13 classics teacher, Dr. Barnes, did more to awaken my interest in the conditions of the Roman poor than I could expect. My family, who put up with me as I locked myself in my office and wrote, deserve particular gratitude.

INDEX

Index

US Constitution, 12

Vergunteius, Lucius, 97, 135-
136
Verres, 65, 77-79, 81, 121
Via Aurelia, 163
Via Cassia, 159, 162
Via Flaminia, 159
Volscii, 112
voting, 3-4, 9-10, 14-15, 23,
62, 88, 111-112, 131, 155